Old Harry's
Dog-Watch

David.

Happy Christmas.
This is just something
which may make you
smile! The other
I will get to Northside.

Love
Pirie

Old Harry's Dog-Watch

The Funny Thing About Cruising ...

Des Sleightholme

Illustrations by the author

ADLARD COLES NAUTICAL
London

Published 1996 by Adlard Coles Nautical
an imprint of A & C Black (Publishers) Ltd
35 Bedford Row, London WC1R 4JH

ISBN 0–7136–4508–3

A CIP catalogue record for this book is available from the
British Library.

Typeset in 11/13 Photina by Falcon Oast Graphic Art
Printed and bound in Great Britain by
The Cromwell Press, Melksham, Wiltshire

Contents

The following pieces are reprinted here with the kind permission of *Yachting Monthly*.

Preface

I find it sobering to reflect that there are folk who are approaching their fortieth year, who are tinting their grey bits and run company cars, who were howling for a nappy change when I first began writing about Old Harry and generally taking the mickey out of sailing.

For this is my great passion, taking the mick, poking fun at the po-faced side of yachting. I have been taken to task by readers many times for my ribaldries, and I can confess with a certain shy pride to having been reported to the Press Council for my derogatory jokes about women. Said this lady, 'I discriminated sexually' (which sounds vaguely as if it ought to be fun but isn't). I did a bit of research and found that I had extracted the you-know-what from sailing women eight times in my last four articles and twenty-five times in the case of men. The case was dropped.

I don't spare myself either Mi'Lud; my own misfortunes and inadequacies provide me with even more fun to be poked and many instances are to be found in the following collection. The battle with a Moss Bros hire suit in a gent's toilet, the rigours of being an after-dinner speaker, tapping one's pipe out in the Point's Trophy Salver on the top table, etc – not funny at the time but rich material later.

Now, long in retirement and still longer in the tooth, one might perhaps expect me to sit nodding over my bread-and-milk, beaming around at the world with a certain benignity, mellowed and kindly. Perhaps my smile might be a touch rueful now that my long and athletic stride has been reduced to the rocking shuffle of a clockwork duck, and now that my sailing days are over.

I sit in my favourite spot on the headland watching the yachts go by, a faithful old dog at my side, bored out of his skull. Far, far below, like a chip of wood, like some delicately winged moth fluttering on the face of the sea, there lies a small sloop. Her crew have managed to hour-glass their spinnaker which is dancing a merry jig around the crosstrees. Will it foul? Will it? Yes and, 'Oh you pillocks', I howl with delight. Mellow benignity? Oh sure.

Oh I must go down to the sea again
To sail o'er the wind and the surf
Though I'm not all that keen
If you see what I mean
But I must get my money's worth

In much the same way that the sound of a tap running can have a dramatic effect upon the bladder, so also the sharing of a night watch can open the floodgates of conversation.

The 8 pm to midnight watch is favourite. Down below the rest of the crew is replete with supper, a nourishing quagmire of tinned stewed steak, peas, beans and spuds which requires the minimum of utensils and intelligence to prepare. They are getting their heads down, grimly intent upon getting some sleep in readiness for later watches. They lie wide awake and fuming as the cockpit raconteurs converse resonantly.

Candidates for crewing vacancies should by rights fill out a questionnaire about their conversational prowess. They could be given a rating. 'Ah here's a Common Agricultural Policy,' an owner will muse, flipping through a wad of applications. Or 'There's a Bring Back the Birch and a couple of Ban the Bypasses'. He'll settle for an applicant renowned for his interminable humorous anecdotes sans punch-lines, as having a beneficial and sophorific effect on those below, who are just embarking upon their first good nightmare.

Oratory lasts until the first midnight chill, then there is a rallying of ghastly jollity as the next watch, socked-out and zombie-like, takes over, after which any jollity is entirely absent.

At 2 am just let anybody ask me if I enjoy Brahms . . . just let them try it that's all. I'm warning you!

'Fresh delights unfold around every bend, eh Desmond!'

1

'It's Three O'clock and You're On!'

Percy's great moon face appears out of the darkness in the companionway. 'Skipper, skipper I think I've got Beachy Head,' he announces, as though confessing to some private and embarrassing scalp condition. Father, who not an hour earlier has explained with the utmost kindness that he can be called for any reason, any reason at all, comes down off the astral plane as though betrayed by a faulty loft ladder. He rears up in his bunk. There is a dull resonance as of a water melon encountering a mallet, and he falls back making laughable gobbling noises.

He is not the most patient of men, as evidenced in the past by the succession of alarm clocks flattened by his flailing fist. With the aid of the duty torch Percy examines the Master's ravaged features at close range, thereby putting a sock on next year's invitation and coming perilously close to winning himself a martyr's crown.

Notwithstanding the Master's hunger for knowledge regarding the safe progress of his vessel, a crew must exercise some judgement as to the quality of the information he is about to pass on. The news that 'I have Sovereign bearing 0-fife-0' fluted down by our tyro may be considered a frivolous reason for shaking the old man out of his first nightmare when the Newhaven Ferry, unnoticed, is barrelling up the wake at 25 knots.

The use of a voicepipe between helmsman and owner's berth might seem a sensible answer to the problem of communication, but it is of questionable value.

'How's your head, helmsman?' raps the owner on a note of reproof.

'Oh a bit better thank you,' rejoins Percy, gratified. 'The old tum-tum isn't quite right yet but …' At that point the voicepipe straightens up like a striking cobra under the quality and force of the vituperation pouring from the mouthpiece.

Of equal threat to shipboard harmony is the owner who, having announced that he may 'put his head down for half an hour and call me, etc, etc', then proceeds to pop up and down like a funfair target. This makes the crew feel about as useful as a mantelpiece full of ornaments.

Conversely, course and speed are of little importance to some crews and the ship might as well be in dry dock for all they care. The helm becomes the social nub with the helmsman/woman masterminding the conversation. 'Well you know I'm not the one for gossip', says Sandra, resting her *en bon point* on the top spokes, 'but he was in there for three hours and I mean how long does it take to read a meter?' She bangs the helm over. She has been leaving a wake like a doctor's signature and the horizon disappears in a blur.

Any hope the owner may cherish of bringing back a few jugs in the unrated cruiser class are short-lived.

'Let Gerald steer for a bit, he's looking a shade peaky,' comes the compassionate cry, steering being well recognised for its therapeutic qualities. It is like suggesting the Red Arrows be replaced by yogic fliers to cut costs. It yields half a mile of seismographic wake followed by a bout of very vocal vomiting.

During a race an on-coming watch cannot wait to get up there. Down below, in a windmilling *mêlée* of arms and legs, they are getting their oilies on as the yacht lurches into the night with a series of shattering jolts.

'Must be all of Force 7,' notes Fwank to Twiston appreciatively. 'Hope it's a dead beat what? Haw, haw, haw,' ripostes Jeremy. They will immediately re-trim all the sheets and then perch in a salt-blasted row along the weather rail. The off-going crowd, spouting water from every buttonhole like municipal water-carts, kick off boots, shuck oily tops and crawl dutifully into windward bunks, there to roost precariously. The ship is tacked. They transfer to the new windward bunks with all the dedication of Easter penitents.

On the other hand, when your cruiser watch goes on duty there is a craven rush for the shelter of the dodger, last man out being helmsman. The off-going watch will have spent the past crawling hour in monosyllabic ill humour. Now, suddenly, all is sweetness and light, jokes are cracked and it would seem that they've had her up to 7 knots in the past hour. They have been thinking about putting a reef in and changing the headsail, but decided to wait and see what the next lot thought.

'We've got Start Point for you,' they add, as though offering some mouth-watering treat. 'Psaaw!' comments the new lot, setting about altering all the sheet settings.

The relief watch is slow to muster at the best of times, even when the ship is prattling over a sea of beaten silver and everybody up there is marvelling at the wonders of creation. 'By God, a king's ransom couldn't buy this,' says Father, eyes aloft, watching the slender, etc, etc tracing its starry course, etc, etc. Somewhere out there comes a gull's lonely cry. 'Hear that gull's lonely cry?' notes Father. A trawlerman, cursing bitterly, helm hard over, receives a pint of tea down the yawning chasm of his trousers.

Watching the emergence of the relief watch is like keeping vigil on a badger set. 'Ssh, look, here's one'. A shy creature thrusts a questing muzzle out into the night air. A watch can sometimes be enticed out by placing a handful of mixed nuts and raisins on the top step.

Not even a desperate cry for all hands on deck can be guaranteed effective. The ship may be on her beam ends, the anchor adrift and hammering its way through the deck; the jib has unrolled, the mainsail has split from luff to leech, the mate has rolled his club tie in with the genoa sheet and the skipper is grabbing at his teeth as they surge up and down the sidedeck.

Below, the call is heard with mixed incredulity and hurt feelings; there is no need for that tone of voice. Jerome wonders whether this is the time to try his new thermal undies,

Shane is searching for a woolly hat, Chesney comes back for a clean hanky.

Sleepers should be approached gingerly, like some firework, the fuse of which, has unaccountably gone out. It is safer to favour the method of waking used by some forward-thinking youth detention centres, which is to blow gently into the ear. The immediate thrusting of a pint of scalding tea into the numbed grasp of your relief goes far in calming natural wrath. He sits staring into it as though divining the future, pendulous lower lip swaying with the ship, eyes blank as pebbles.

Not that the rigours of getting kitted out down below are ever fully appreciated by the novice until finally faced by them. Figures bicycle for balance on the edges of leeward settees, from the loo comes the sound of thuds, jangles and curses as though somebody was trying to saddle up a bucking bronco and Agnes, having got into it all, has a sneaking

5

feeling that she ought to have gone somewhere first. It is like knights saddling up for Agincourt. Resentful eyes watch this little tableau from the companionway.

Olga, the Swedish au pair, five foot four, stretch tank-top, arrives on deck moments after Mother, who is sensibly trousered and with her storm front fully zipped. It seems that the poor kid isn't feeling good and that Father will take her in his watch, where he can keep his eye on her (it hasn't been off her since she came on board). She finds herself in Mother's watch, where she gets the pull-yourself-together-girl treatment – perplexing advice for one with a poor command of the language.

The whole ship revolves about Father's undoubted superiority in matters marine, a fact which gives him a certain Thespian outlook and temperament. The preservation of his night vision is an aspect painfully played up on every occasion. That and the efficacy of colonic irrigation (which smacks of sluices and rice paddies, but is in fact something medical and nasty) are his favourite topics. Percy unwisely begins hunting around in the cockpit with a pen torch such as a surgeon might use to look you-know-where. 'Agggh my night vision, my night vision!' howls the Master, groping around dramatically. We're in for a bad night.

Few will ever forget the rich experience of a night watch in Old Harry's converted Hake-dragger. With paraffin side-lights gouting black and stinking smoke, Norman (who should never have had the fried bread) breathes economically, remembers it, and groans. He will be on until breakfast time; he shudders in anticipation.

At this point the Master's head emerges from the hatch, pipe belching smoke and sparks like the old Flying Scot leaving a tunnel. A hot waft flows up from the galley where a pan chuckles maniacally and nutritiously. 'There'll be a nice bit o' pig's cheek for when you come off son,' he promises. Strung over the lee rail the yellow seat of Norman's oily trousers caught in the baleful light of the binnacle looks like some strange sunrise.

6

When saddled with a crew of mediocre talents, Father may go into his on-call mode, which allows him to hog the quarter-berth all night, dispensing wisdom while everybody else takes turns sitting in the rain.

Just occasionally, and with a crew of peculiar nautical stupidity and ineptitude, the only solution may be for him to do the whole lot himself. At ten o'clock, like putting the cat out, up he goes with his pockets full of provender as though facing hibernation. Down below, resting at ease in the knowledge that he is up there, wrestling with problems, the ship's company snores softly. Father, a munching silhouette, stares with resentment at the warm glow of the open hatch and wrestles with his problems. 'Shall I have the Mars bar at midnight or the apple?' he agonises.

Shockcord or 'bungee' can be habit-forming. You can become hooked on finding new uses for it. Aboard a boat it has endless uses. When we recall that yachties are also butchers, bakers, candlestick makers and brokers as well, it naturally follows that they will find fresh tasks for it to perform ashore.

And hence the pensioner presenting her Gyro cheque at the Post Office counter. WHAM! Down comes the Position Closed sign like Traitor's Gate on care-worn fingers; shockcord. Or take poor little pussy tottering around in circles with eyes crossed, tragic evidence of miscalculation in the repair of a cat-flap.

The medical profession is particularly plagued by yachting doctors who suffer from shockcord syndrome. 'I think we'll have to put our leg in traction Mrs Muffin,' laughs a surgeon doing bed-rounds. He has cocked up a hip replacement and it has turned out to be a bit on the short side. A nurse hurries up with an assortment of pullies and sandbags. 'Thank you nurse but I prefer to use my own system,' he says in clipped tones, proceeding to rig up a bit of the 14mm stuff. 'There you go then!' He laughs cheerily, applying tension. With a whoop Mrs Muffin shoots out of sight beneath the bedclothes like a crash-diving submarine.

Perils of a Bungee Boggin

Every boat I have owned has been strung up with bits of shockcord – of bungee rubber. Under way in a breeze they twanged and hummed away like a Chinese orchestra. Or you'd get naturalists calling for silence with upraised forefinger. 'Listen!' they would rap, 'that's a snipe dumming, by heaven!' But it wasn't; it was Old Sleightholme in some fat little cruiser pounding along on a broad reach.

I have always been inventive. I get it from my Father who had it in his jeans – as dear old Bill Beavis used to say. Give Father a few old mousetraps, some rubber bands and a tin of carbide and he'd have had a man on the moon years ahead of his time.

It wasn't just afloat that I explored the wonderful world of bungee. I made this cat-scarer for the garden. A length of bungee was stretched under hellish strain and held by a hair trigger mechanism crossing the route followed daily by a neighbour's spraying tom-cat. Activated, it went off THRRRAPP! And hurled a can of water. Joyce's rake did it. 'OUT' she snarled, 'I want it out and NOW!'

In one boat there was this row of little slit portholes like letter boxes. When alongside, a viewer from without was treated to an intriguing and segmented view of anyone who happened to be *en déshabillé* below; it was irresistible to jig-saw buffs. I made these little lids held by bungee. They were a bit tricky, though, and kept falling off. On the quayside, frowning observers with heads cocked sideways wrestled with the challenge.

I suppose later owners of my boats must be old men now, wiser old men with missing front teeth and cauliflower ears. There were the saloon tables that leapt to their feet like subalterns when the Colonel walks in, locker lids that whammed shut, rigging frapping lines that hummed like disturbed hornets, and the cooker grill-pan, immovable by those not privy to its ingenuity, filled the air with billowing clouds of burned toast.

There was also my sheet winch self-tailer. A length of bungee anchored low aft in the cockpit terminated in a Clam Cleat which, at full stretch, could be clapped on the tail of the sheet. (Yes, I thought that would astonish you.) It had a minor deficiency, however. Any out-for-a-day-sail guest lodged aft out of the way was right in line. Very rarely the thing let go and your guest, carolling like a lark, would zoom upright clutching ... well you know ... and rigid with agony.

The impact of bungee rubber on Old Harry was profound. His genius for improvisation is well known; for example his stair-lift for the elderly and infirm (not widely accepted due to problems of undue acceleration) made a great impact.

Assembled from such homely components as half a supermarket trolley, a quantity of twisting, dripping garden hosepipe and an old hot water tank suspended on pullies from a back bedroom window, the Social Services lady in the porkpie hat who came to inspect the novelty was hugely struck by it – but then she *had* been warned about the descending tank.

The wide use of rubber aboard his vessel leaves it humming like a hornet's nest following the exploratory prod of the rambler's walking stick ('What busy little creatures they are Muriel.') Scorning the chandler's costly products, he looks elsewhere for elasticity. Nocturnal outrages involving garden clothes-lines and the vandalism of *certain garments* threw the Neighbourhood Watch into turmoil and ladies stopped running for buses.

Bicycle inner tubes provided another rich source of supplies. 'Goodness just look at the time. Choir practice!' cries the vicar, keen to distance himself from the Widow Watkins and her Various Veins. 'Never mind, I'll be on the flat all the way,' he forecasts accurately. He judders off, dog-collar shuttling up and down his glottis like a valve tappet.

There is no limit to the things you can do with a bit o' bungee. Take bunks. You can make a sort of trampoline with bungee. Going to windward in a bit of a lump, your occupant is shooting up and down as if riddling cinders. The original Sleightholme seaberth was something else. There may still be those alive who will recall what it was like because I wrote about it. There was a strange total silence from the readership.

What you need in harbour is a firm settee at normal level, but at sea you need a sort of trough. I had a hinged flap

running full length to which was attached one edge of the bunk's bungee base. When the flap was raised the bungee went slack; when the flap was forced downwards, however, it drew the bungee drum-tight. The flap was held in this position by a brass turnbuckle, a device which was on a par with securing a bull-pen with knicker elastic.

We'd had a hard sail. Now, at anchor, it was time for peace after stormy seas and the blessed benison of sleep. The others had turned in. 'Ahhh!' I sighed contentedly, flinging myself down on my settee berth. There was a shattering bang. The heads of aroused sleepers thudded against sidedecks. I vanished into my trough with a howl while the brass turnbuckle zinged and pinged, ricocheting around the cabin, and a nervous crew-member began struggling into his lifejacket.

Bungee offers special advantages in the form of quick-release devices. In one of my boats a quick tug at a red knob brought about a sort of convulsion on the aft pulpit. Bungee bands flew apart, releasing lifebuoy, danbuoy, automatic light and a coil of floating line, all calculated either to stun or strangle the casualty in the water. Nor was that all; the tugging of two more red knobs to port and starboard caused lead-weighted footropes to drop down the topsides while – activated by bungee – the guardrails and dodgers shot forwards and down, leaving a bare sidedeck.

It was like a Q-ship opening up on a U-boat. All it lacked was the deadly muzzle of a four-pounder barking its vengeful challenge, the snap of a battle ensign and a crash-diving sub. Thankfully, the arrangement was never put to the test, but I lived in dread of inquisitive fingers.

Then there was the unpleasant business of 'the boggin line'. As readers will need no telling, a boggin line is what secures the rudder blade of a Thames Barge to one side, bracing against the wheel or tiller lashing and thereby holding all firm. I had a bungee boggin line which led to the sidedeck very unobtrusively; it was meant to cut out rudder movement on the mooring and thus reduce pintle chafe.

I told my old mate he could borrow the boat whenever he wanted, so he did. I had forgotten to warn him about the boggin line. Whistling in carefree manner he hoisted main and jib, threw off the mooring and sauntered aft to the tiller. Arthur, taking first pull at the sword in the stone, must have felt a similar emotion. His smile snapped off. Relentlessly the bows began to pay off as, with helm immovably hard over, the yacht went into her first uncontrolled gybe. She came whizzing up into the wind, went through stays and bore off once more, while he cursed in a mounting falsetto and wrenched and tugged. He had three flying gybes and an equal number of tacks to his score before he managed to drag the mainsail half down and boot the anchor overboard.

Even at the sunset of my life, a bread-and-milk wallah with all passion spent, my fascination with bungee continues. On Wednesday mornings, dustbin day and an event of significance in a quiet village, the air rings to the merry laughter of the refuse operatives as my bungee-powered dustbin lid snaps down on their fingers.

I hate litter. In order to pick up the Snicker wrappers and crisp packets that line the coastal walks, I have equipped one of my walking sticks with a species of copper dentures. Operated by a finger string and with a bungee return spring, I can stab and grab with deadly efficiency. 'Don't catch his eye, dear!' mothers caution their young as I go mumbling and snapping by.

And latest of all is the Sleightholme Dog-Stick Launcher. If you own one of those dogs that are paranoid about having sticks thrown, you can end up with a strained right arm – I have overcome this hazard. I have cut a notch in the end of his stick and seized an eye in the end of a short length of bungee. I can project a stick twice as far, which means it takes him twice as long to retrieve it, ergo half the number of throws per walk.

I hit an early snag. The dog was conditioned to react Pavlov-fashion to the raised arm. When I discharged the stick from waist level he just remained on his marks. He never saw it go. 'Fetch it then you cretin!' I screamed. He rose slowly to his feet and looked me over sneeringly. I had to retrieve it myself.

(By the same author: *Boys' Bumper Bungee Annual, Bungee and the Church Today, Bungee and Marital Harmony, Make Your Own Athletic Underwear.*)

nly once have I been wrecked. *That's to say, had to abandon ship amidst grinding timbers, thundering waves, racing gibbous moon and all that Poldark stuff. In fact it was about as life-threatening as an all-parents' sack race.*

There was Richard the owner, Helen, and me, and we'd grounded near the top of the tide. A local fisherman was booked to tow us off when the flood had made sufficiently, which would be near enough midnight, and, meanwhile we laid out our best bower across the sands to seaward. Then the weather went bad.

By the time we were beginning to float we were being hammered like a tympanum. Bang, crash, bang. 'She can't take this for long!' said Richard. 'Don't worry darling, I can stick it.' Helen cried bravely.

'Not you. The boat!' he corrected. 'Oh. Well thank you very much I'm sure!' She said, a bit huffy.

In the light of a scudding moon we saw the fisherman arrive, take stock, and making the wash-out signal he departed bedwards. Doubtless he expected that we'd wade ashore, as indeed did I. 'I stay with my ship,' proclaimed Richard stoutly. 'I stay with you darling.' Helen minced. 'Oh s**t,' I said.

We went below, closed the companionway doors, and sat in a row on the settee to wait for the tide and Richard's gin supply to ebb. The yacht now fully afloat was hurling back on her anchor – which was secured to our stern – with a series of shattering lunges. Waves were hitting our transom stern like gun shots and the spray swept our decks.

Suddenly there was a roaring, a great boom, and the companionway doors burst inwards followed by a solid wall of water. There we sat, knee-deep, clutching our gin-and-seawaters. 'We must abandon!' cried Richard, and not before time in my opinion.

'I can't swim,' Helen told us belatedly. It was my finest hour. I stiffened my upper lip. 'I . . . I'll go first . . . with a line,' I declared.

'No. I am the skipper and Helen is my girl!' Richard said – to my huge relief. I made an 'aw shucks' gesture and stood down.

On deck and up for'd it was a wild Wagnerian scene. All it lacked was a huge soprano with horns and wearing saucepan lids. Cloud rack raced and tore. We were surrounded by white water and the line of the shore was sixty yards away.

Richard recommended his soul to his Maker like it was some sort of new washing powder, and tying the end of a line about his middle he plunged head-first overboard. Never one to miss an opportunity, I grappled with Helen. We saw Richard floundering, then standing on the shore jumping up and down and waving in an odd manner.

I secured the other end of the line around Helen's waist, taking my time for it was a rewarding job. 'Get on with it then!' she said tartly. I gave her a good shove. Richard was hauling away with vigour. She went shorewards like a gunboat going into action, for she was a well endowed lass. Then there they both were jumping up and down and waving.

I was alone. My face worked convulsively. 'Gawd bless'ee lad,' I told myself, recommending my soul and so on. My hard, lean young body cleft the raging waters like a javelin. ZONK.

ZONK? Yes mate, zonk because the water was hardly more than thigh-deep. I trudged shorewards.

A Dribble Under the Futtocks

Prehistoric man, astride his log, bandy-legged and permanently soaked to the knees, was probably the last mariner not threatened by the prospect of sinking – that is until today's multihuller, astride his inverted vessel, bandy-legged, permanently soaked to the knee and jubilantly unsinkable.

We don't give a lot of thought to the possibility of sinking, except for now and again at 0200 on a black and windy solo watch, when every wave that heaves up under the lee bow becomes a submerged container full of export garden rollers.

Today's mariners are less worried by hull leaks than their forebears, who hid their fears behind a vast and weird nomenclature. A bad leak could be *fothered* with a *thrum mat* and lesser leaks could be *maured*, a process in which a bucket of sawdust is thrust down under the leaking hull in the expectation that leaking seams would suck in beneficial quantities of the dust, which would then swell and so on. Anyone who has attempted, clandestinely, to dump gash overboard and then tried to poke it out of sight with the boathook, will appreciate the degree of skill required for this strategy.

The belief that a boat should leak enough to 'keep her sweet' once bedevilled your boat-hunting novice. Old Harry with a bargain for sale was always ready with advice for the beginner.

Percy cocks an attentive ear to the sloshing and gurgling sounds beneath his feet. Consoled by this abundant promise of a wholesome hull, he hands over his wad with the innocence of some punter buying a Rolex in Paddington Station gents.

'A couple of strokes at turn o' watch and you'll be laughin',' promises the vendor, hinting at crews rendered helpless with mirth. The truth will out. The pump-work in store for our luckless tyro is to develop his upper torso to the stage where he will have the lolloping gait and swinging arms of Quasimodo.

Owners had their favourite recipes for stopping hull leaks. 'Have you tried porridge oats and soft soap?' enquires one, generously sharing a well guarded secret. 'No' but I've got this nasty little dribble under my futtocks that is responding well to ground rice pudding and beeswax!' enthuses the other, to a spellbound audience of fellow bus passengers.

There is also your 'hull-integrity' buff. 'I'll not have them drilling holes in *my* hull!' he trumpets, as if besieged by a squad of boatyard mateys in jungle-green boiler suits brandishing hammer-drills. With an air of defiance he proceeds to wash up the breakfast crocks in a bucket, which he then empties over the side with a tinkling of teaspoons.

Most yachts are riddled with holes like a prime Stilton, with the loo installation contributing generously to the total. The only solution is the chemical toilet – the updated 'thunderbox' dear to our ancestors. It necessitates nocturnal trips ashore to dispose of the *sealed container*.

'Excuse me, Sir!' barks HM Customs Officer, triumphantly stepping out of concealment. 'I must ask you what you have in your bag?' It is a great moment for our yachtsman.

The mechanical sea toilet is the bane and dread of the tyro, living afloat for the first time. It seems that one cannot have an ordinary, simple bowel movement without manipulating all manner of levers, cocks, pumps and gate valves. It is like starting up a fairground steam organ. All it lacks is the smirking plaster shepherdess banging cymbals.

'Shhh, I thought I heard a little tinkle!' says Blanche, raising the cautionary finger.

Father is on to it like a hound from the slips. He wrenches open the loo door. His bowl it doth run over. He proceeds to give the most moving performance of his thespian career afloat. With his features wrenched into a mask of intolerable suffering, he calls upon his Maker to bear witness. 'Why!' he flutes. 'We could all have been drowned as we slept!' The unlikely event of people sleeping blissfully while being immersed slowly in a freezing English Channel escapes him. The guilty party will bear the mark of Cain for life, pointed out in the street in whispers, as might a reprieved mass-murderer.

When it comes to sinking, boats need no help from us. They can manage very nicely unaided. Just as the humble bank vole, toiling away underground at the plastic liner to an ornamental garden pool, can turn that charming feature into a puddle of stinking mud and dead goldfish, so can the yacht left on moorings provide a rude surprise for her owners returning at the weekend.

Father gets out of the car and shades his eyes. 'Oh, deary me!' he chuckles with good-natured tolerance for the ineptitudes of fellow mariners. 'Some poor swine is in for a nasty shock, eh?' He surveys the distant mast, 1.82m (6ft) of which is protruding from the water. His smile slowly stiffens as though it had been varnished on. His Adam's apple rises and falls once … 'Did we leave the burgee up?' he asks generally, in stricken tones.

There are such time-honoured sources of leak as the sterngland. Like some holy well, deep in its grotto, haunt of naiad and shy kingfisher, it never runs dry and is seldom visited. The ritual of 'hardening it down' is one bitterly familiar to many a sailing wife, whose job it will be to hand tools to her spouse and suffer his clicks and sighs at being handed the wrong one.

The disembodied knees, shins and toe-blasted deck shoes, visible in the deep and shadowy recesses of the quarterberth, are not the grisly evidence that some maniacal meat-saw killer has been at work, but father attending to the sterngland.

The time will come when merely screwing down the greaser and causing more worms of grease to writhe into the bilge is not enough; it will have to be re-packed. The shaft has been rattling around like a walking stick down a gutter. Torch in mouth and one-handed, ring spanner at full stretch of finger tips, father howls for yet another as it joins the rest in the deep vee of the sterntuck. Short of training his five-year-old on a Lego mock-up in the cupboard under the kitchen sink, he will have to 'get the yard in' which, for your budget owner, is near to blasphemy.

The boatyard, forbidden by the Factories Act to stuff apprentices down black holes, as if rabbiting with a ferret, solves the problem by lifting out the engine – a process which will cost about the same as a gas chairman's salary.

Another ritual of modern yachting relates to the 'log

impeller skin fitting', a term smacking of cosmetic surgery and a bit of slack around your wattles. At the end of a cruise, and prior to leaving the boat, it has to be *unshipped*, an exercise akin to applying a thumb over one of the mighty fountains of Versailles.

It's a chore traditionally reserved for father, who privately dreads it. The job involves unscrewing and withdrawing the impeller and replacing it with a screwcap. With the cabin sole up, father, sleeves rolled, kneels by the hole as if in deep mourning at a graveside. Blanche stands by with basin, swabs and a towel. He has thought out a new system. This time he will hold the cap in his right hand while unscrewing the impeller with his left. He slackens off a few turns, grits his teeth and the old familiar spluttering howl of dismay rises from the forehatch as he lifts his ravaged and dripping features to the light.

The throbbing heart of a boat used to be the bilge pump. In days when deckheads dripped like Mother Shipton's Grotto, and hull seams munched their oakum as if it were some new health breakfast cereal, you relied on your bilge pump.

Typical might be Old Harry's converted winkle walloper, a vessel with the windward qualities of a nun's bonnet. Although never a class of craft to quicken the pulse and bring a lump to the throat (apart from the occasion when he boiled the sink plug with the potatoes), she had a pump barrel that could woo a potholer and a pumpwell with an echo. You had to lower a canary in a cage prior to groping for the lost starting handle; if you'd fallen down, you would have needed a decompression stop on the way up.

The pump handle, shipped in a deck socket next to the black maw of the open barrel, looked like an iron heron peering down in expectation of being richly rewarded. It was never disappointed. Slurp-clunk, slurp-clunk went the pump, and at each stroke a reeking black soup burped up over the sidedeck. It was peppered with dead beetles, lentils, dog-ends, blanket fluff and unidentifiable gobbets of corruption.

Not so your light displacement go-go boat of today, in which a pint of water goes everywhere, like a puddle next to a bus stop. None of your cast iron artefacts here, oh no. In a pump well the size of a dolly's bath there is an electronic sensor. Like some electronic big toe, recoiling from contact with rising water, it motivates a softly humming pump that quickly copes with the emergency. Excepting just that once …

The sleeper, alerted by the chilliness of his buttocks, awakens and raises himself upon one elbow. As though taking the salute at some Naval review, he watches his shoes go floating past.

He looked familiar. He caught my eye and it was too late. I racked my brains to remember his name. 'Hello there,' I said, nod, nod, smile, smile.

'Now then,' he said, smile-nod.

We confronted one another, beaming, rocking on our heels. Who the hell was he?

'How are you getting on then?' I asked idiotically. It seemed he was getting on fine, which was more than I was. We both studied the ceiling and I whistled a few bars of nothing. Who the hell was he?

He said, 'What have you been up to lately then?' I said, 'Oh, you know, this and that.' We went back to ceiling study and I whistled another bar or two.

I asked, angling, 'Let's see, when did we meet last? A year or more?'

He frowned. 'Oh phew. It must be. A year – maybe more.'

'At least.' I countered.

'Seems longer,' I said after a pause. He agreed that it seemed longer and didn't time fly eh? We returned to our ceiling and whistling. He cracked first.

'Let's face it,' he said, 'you don't know me and I haven't the faintest bloody idea who you are!'

I grinned. 'Let's have a drink.'

Handing the Nuts Around

The thing to be borne in mind when inviting total strangers aboard for drinks is that it's not so much a matter of whether they'll come as whether they'll go.

Usually it is the old man who hands out the random invitations after a survey of the burgees and what's on offer. He remembers to mention the fact about half an hour before guests are due. Lady-wife, predictably, throws a wobbly. 'But we haven't any peanuts!' she cries aghast, implying that casual guests, like some monstrous blue tits, will immediately hang upside-down in the rigging and wait to be fed. In near-panic she begins smearing little bits of toast with Marmite.

Invitations to drinks must be worded with caution. Make them sound too formal and guests turn up in bow-ties and boat cloaks while you are still scuttling around in your shattered Bermudas topping up sump oil. On the other hand, a too-casual note, 'Feel like coming aboard for a drink?' implies that they are dying of thirst with blackened lips and lolling tongues. It also determines whether they rate the soggy crisps or the Twiglets.

Strict timing is vital. An invitation issued to your non-sailing couple must not trespass on Shipping Forecast time. Father sits poised over his pad like a sprinter on his marks. 'Here is the Shipping Forecast,' says the announcer superfluously.

'Yoo hoo!' comes a voice from the pontoon alongside. 'Cooeee! Is anybody in?'

Father calls upon his Maker through gritted teeth, which is not that easy. He snaps his pencil and retracts his neck like a tortoise in the vain hope of becoming invisible.

'Shout again darling, I'm sure there's someone in it,'

comes a male voice. 'First,' tantalises the announcer, 'there are some gale warnings ...'

With that Mother makes her entry, bustling up from the loo where she has been busy with blusher and eyeshadow. She's overdone it again and looks like an ornamental pheasant. She passes her crouching spouse, hissing at him like a gander and snapping on her hostess smile. 'Oh gush, gush, gush,' she exclaims, 'Do come aboard, gush, gush!'

Father snaps off the radio with a shuddering sigh, brutally wronged and looking it. He is a martyr to duty and don't blame him if there are hurricanes, freak tidal waves and waterspouts off West Wittering, and don't blame him, either, if he hasn't laid out kedges, lashed down his lazarette and sent down his topmasts. What matters is passing the peanuts and keeping what's-his-name's glass topped up.

If you don't want your guests to become lodgers keep them on deck. Let them go below at your peril. Once a guest gets his hooter down the companionway it's like trying to get rid of carrot-fly. Various strategies for getting shot of them may be attempted, such as sticking a head out and crying 'Look everybody, a hoopoo!', or 'Time we polished the clock' or (yawning hugely) 'Oh dear, another early start in the morning.'

Once a guest is well into his saga of iniquitous harbour masters, he's harder to shift than gravy stains on a rented dinner jacket. A sulphur candle might do it, possibly a three-star red or a dry powder extinguisher discharged up the kilt. Failing all, changing into pyjamas and setting the alarm clock is the last hope.

Cruising friendships struck up in the marina ablutions, or on the strength of owning boats of the same class, can be tenuous. After all, you don't shower them with your nuts because she's wearing the same C&A sweater. Get it wrong and they may lay waste your drinks locker like Drake sacking Cadiz. They may even arrive with The Lad in tow – 14 years old, 6ft in his gigantic trainers, ears like wing mirrors and a baseball cap seemingly spot-welded to his scalp.

23

'*You have no Coke!*' He accepts squash like a Friend of the Earth accepting leaded petrol, and thereafter sits sighing and consulting his gigantic, digital, multi-face, diver's watch, set to countdown mode.

Keep them off the hard stuff, but don't hide the gin in the chart drawer, where it will come to light later when showing him the easy way through the Raz de Seine – a disturbing reflection on your navigational integrity.

Whether to give them the good stuff or the supermarket jumbo offer in the plastic carboy will depend on gut reaction. Never apologise for the rough stuff. A nervous host may take the precaution of decanting it into a nice bit of lead crystal (a chipped enamel jug might be more appropriate), but there is a classic procedure to be followed. Pour the 'him' of the couple a half glass. 'I'd like your opinion of this,' you say, looking at him steadily.

While a sincere and honest man might stagger upright clawing at his throat before rushing on deck to vomit noisily down your topsides, you have, at a single stroke, buttered up a male ego and elevated him to the status of connoisseur. He will have done the wine tasting evening at the village hall so he'll give you the full performance. 'Aaahumph!' he says, cheeks sucked in as if his dentures were in peril. Fighting for time he holds it up to the light. 'Wheeeuff. It's very … well definitely … very er, yes!' he sums up helpfully.

Stick to the intimate foursome. Cockpit drinking for larger parties calls for larger cockpits; otherwise you've got guests perched all over your coachroof like migrating starlings. You'll also get them lining the narrowest of sidedecks, guardrails pressing backs of knees, a fistful of nuts in one hand and a sixth top-up in the other just as the harbour ferry goes by. 'Why, look Mummy, a water ballet,' exclaim delighted onlookers as guests perform a backward somersault in perfect unison.

More than six at a go in your smaller cruiser is pushing it. With knees fringing the cockpit like big game at a small waterhole, the normal cocktail party convention wherein

everybody stands up amidst a superfluity of chairs is impracticable. Guests must remain seated while hosts circulate acrobatically as if feeding chicks in a nest, the one gazing up the nostrils of the others who, in their turn, are fated to study the bald patches, as though engaged in an aerial investigation of crop-circles.

It does little for the thrust and parry of intelligent conversation. A mahogany man with ear tufts like a red squirrel stares up at the burgee, desperate for inspiration. 'What's that you're wearing then?' he enquires of the owner's cousin Hilda, sitting next to him and only down for the day. It's a little woolly she knitted from a pattern in *Woman's Weekly*, and if he likes it she'll lend it to him.

Old Harry, living fossil, champion of the Rippingill cooker and to club social secretaries what woolly aphid is to the fruit grower, entertains on a generous scale which leaves in his wake veteran guests crouched in the shadows, rocking to and fro while clutching their temples.

Scorning 'foreign muck' he sets much store by his home-made peapod hock-style or the rhubarb burgundy-style – a beverage which has contributed to rocketing absenteeism by those confined to their bathrooms the following day.

Laughing off the expense, he offers his guests a bewildering choice of comestibles. Nuggets of bread pudding and pork dripping vie with crackling and pig's ears. There is a sack of peanuts and nibbles misleadingly labelled 'mixed wild bird food'. 'Come on, don't be frightened to dip in,' he encourages, swiping left and right with his cap at the finches, sparrows and dunnets which surround it.

In happier climes, the on-board barbecue offers new dimensions of hospitality, and still wider scope for disaster. The sheer awfulness of a back patio barbecue in our own brisk latitudes makes the Brit reluctant to try one. Attended by midges and those guests who were too slow to think up an excuse for being elsewhere, we find dad on hands and knees, eyes dark-ringed like a racoon, puffing at the sulky charcoal, watched by guests as prisoners might eye the assembled firing squad.

Later. 'Have another spare rib,' urges our gracious hostess (having more to spare than she knows what to do with). Guests raise protective hands as though warding off evil. Gerald, seated unsuitably on a folding deckchair, eyes his fate from between goose pimpled knees. 'Here's yours then Gerald,' she says, handing him a paper plate stacked high with scorched and congealing gobbets. The plate bends. It is like watching a tipper-truck deliver a load of furnace nuts on a front lawn.

Potential guests should know when to leave. On a first visit, to outlast the Twiglets is to outstay your welcome. Give their wine box a couple of quick bashes, grab a handful of nuts, see where he stows his EPIRB, then it's 'Goodness, look at the time!' and on your way.

There is a ritual procedure for leaving, a sort of duet

intoned by guest and host as legs are cocked over guardrails. 'Simply lovely ... delighted we could come ... must visit us.' Hosts wait until guests have their outboard running and 50 yards intervenes before starting to discuss them. It is by now dusk, dew falling and bellies rumbling. It will have to be something on toast.

Oh, we must go down to the sea again
Out on the bounding Main
But be in no doubt
We'll be going flat out
To get the hell off it again.

Most yacht sea-passages, with the exception of ocean voyages, take less than or not much longer than twenty-four hours. You'd think the aim of yachties was to get 'out there' where the wind's like a whetted knife. Not a bit of it. The quicker they can get it over and done with the better. Nab Tower to Cherbourg in only ten hours. Wheee!

Meals en route are a cheerless necessity, munching stolidly out in the cockpit with your hair blown horizontal, chomping on a chicken drumstick or slurping instant soup from a mug while those shipmates of delicate pastel complexion nibble on a biscuit which is devoid of taste, smell or colour.

Feeding, once safely in harbour, becomes a scene of gastronomic madness. Boil-in-the-bag or instant paella (add water and jump clear) need no lauding on my part. There'll be a Lyons tart plus aerosol whipped cream, all washed down with Cote de Tesco and instant coffee which has gone hard in the jar. A cold wash-up in seawater rounds off the evening. Oh what crazy fools!

For novice owners embarking upon their first foreign cruise the annual Club Cruise in Company is the culmination of winter evenings of acheing buttocks on plastic chairs, adult education and a confused concept of magnetic lines of force and who-gives-way-to-whom. Across their charts marches The Rhumb Line, an unbroken series of XXXXs like some monstrous millipede and denoting non-stop position fixing.

Old Harry, self-appointed champion of the novices, never misses these occasions. Disdaining such fripperies as VHF radio and having the sound lungs the Good Lord gave him (an ill-chosen gift if ever there was one) he delivers his nuggets of advice via cupped hands.

Motor-sailing from boat to boat with a tremendous racket punctuated by shattering explosions, he has a word of encouragement for all. 'Don't let your head fall off!' he advises a little man in a cricket sweater who begins neck-circling anxiously (an Algipan rubbing for him that night). 'She's dragging her bustle,' he councils the next. The owner's lady-wife bristles and sits down hastily. The next owner is informed that he has a wrinkled nock and yet another would be well advised to clap a jigger on his foot and swig down. Old Harry leaves a decimated fleet of anxious tyros, stopped, circling or heading for home and the solace of the National Health Service.

Rhumb Goings On

oing foreign is what counts, and it doesn't matter whether you arrive home with bananas ripening in the rigging or six Quimper egg cups and a barometer stuck all over with limpet shells. The important thing is that you've been 'across the other side', an expression which smacks of lowered lights and linked hands around the table.

Your true long-distance sailor can be identified by ragged eyebrows which appear to have been blasted by bird-shot, deep-set, horizon-scanning eyes, and a handbag complexion, features which establish his authenticity like a finger bandage in a home-made bakery bread roll. The modesty of such mariners is insufferable to those of us given to boasting about our Ostend-and-back epics.

'Been far old chap?'

'Bay of Fundy again. And you?'

'Malacca Straits. Ran out of time, I'm afraid.'

Father, fresh home after a night of staring with owlish incomprehension at the lights of thundering container ships, wisely remains silent. Not for him the hiss of coral sand and the tinkle of the gamelan; instead, the cheery greeting of a Dutch bargemaster beaten by a narrow margin to the lock gates.

First time foreign is a truly unforgettable experience. It is the product of long evenings spent with aching buttock on plastic chair being harangued by an instructor who is determined to leave nothing unsaid, no danger uncatalogued, from water-spout to ice-blink, and the effect of sunspots on magnetic compass. Our tyro sets forth in much the same frame of mind as the earliest flat-earth explorers, resignation tempered by gloomy curiosity.

Having taken a last harrowing look at the land as it disappears astern, the empty hours of a maiden crossing pass in heightening tension. Father, navigating non-stop, produces a line on the chart that bristles with positions as if it had been blanket stitched. Using every method available, including Decca, GPS, RDF, DR, prayer and fasting, he eventually raises land ahead.

'Well, there's your Barfleur then!' he announces with pride, as if he'd just that moment fished it piping hot from the oven. 'Another couple of hours and you'll be knocking back the old vang blong.'

It is at this point in my narrative that experienced navigators will pass a weary hand across their eyes and shudder. They know all too well that statements of this kind are about as ill-advised as trying out a funny handshake on the traffic cop who has just shunted you into a lay-by. In fact, in terms of invitation to disaster, it is tantamount to sticking the funnel down the front of your own trousers. It would save a lot of time all round if you waited for the spring ebb to begin and the wind to fall flat, then took your boat a mile downtide of the headland and fed your diesel a generous dose of air bubbles.

The hard truth of the matter is that 'Making the passage

plan' is often the best and certainly most comfortable bit. Seated at the saloon table with Chart No 24 *English Channel to Gibraltar* fully deployed, father becomes master of the oceans, the tides are his kingdom and the billows his slaves; an Olympian figure. 'If you don't want supper, well, that's fine by me,' intones his lady-wife, a bit tight-lipped.

The passage plan is a charming little fiction, a nautical tooth-fairy, Enid Blyton in Docksiders. The dividers stalk unhindered across the chart with the confident aggression of a rambler on a contested footpath. 'By maintaining an average 4 knots, we will be off Cap de la Hague in time to pick up the west-going stream,' trumpets father, rubbing his hands.

What he will pick up is 10 fathoms of drift-net around the fan, a wigging for the lost bread knife and an extra night out.

In theory, he will be darting from waypoint to waypoint as if gathering pollen; in truth his passage plan is likely to come to a shuddering end five miles from departure when the forecast Force 4 reach becomes a Force 5 dead muzzler. Thereafter, two hours on the rocking horse with a cockpit full of people wearing mustard complexions heralds a sharp change of plan, a freeing of sheets and a smart scuttle for the nearest shelter to leeward.

Or a passage plan may get off to an encouraging start, log ticking, DR hiking across the chart and everybody in high spirits, all wearing tomato soup moustaches and exchanging *merci beaucoups* and *pardonezmoi's* in anticipation of an early arrival. Then speed falls to a lumpy 2½ knots. 'We'll give her a touch of engine,' cries dear old dad. Progress becomes a plunging 5 knots flat out and there are gritted teeth all round, with the exception of those which are wisely stowed in a pocket.

This is when 'halfway there' becomes 'halfway back'. Father left in sole command, wrestles with decisions. 'What is best for my crew?' he asks himself rhetorically. 'Whoooop awww,' chorus the bowed heads at the lee rail.

Our frail bark reaches her destination and anchors an

hour before dawn, just as night is diluted by muddy daylight. It is the hour of weary triumph, raw hands grip brimming tot glasses in the steamy warmth of the saloon, fingers rasp stubbled chins (the blokes), and the kettle whistles unattended. It is a time for making rash promises. 'If you like, Skipper ...' says the creep who-only-came-because-Norman-was-having-an-operation, '... if you like, when we've had a bit of kip I'll nip ashore and get some fresh croissants.'

We all know him. He'll lie feigning sleep, as if awaiting the kiss of some fairy prince, until booted into resentful action. Pump the dinghy, lowest spring tide of the year, slipway a Cresta run of black ooze, last year's bakery now a gift shop full of china, wailing women and pictures of the Raz de Sein in a gale. He'll tramp a mile and back to the village, then return to find breakfast over and father fretting to catch the tide.

The final approach to a hitherto unvisited foreign marina is fraught with terror. The helmsman's Adam's apple shuttles up and down like a crow in a chimney, there are clipped commands and the odd clipped earhole. Having a flag in one hand and a bag of trade goods in the other may have been fine for Captain Cook (and he never drew his pension either), but the sight of a semaphoring Harbourmaster wearing a bullet shaped peaked cap would take the pea out of anybody's whistle. He indicates a berth reachable only by mobile crane.

Father clears his throat. There is this trouble with the astern gear. 'Le moteur non marches bloody backwards,' he hails fluently. He notes the narrowing gap between bows, berth and a bill for £500 with the pop-eyed resignation of the hunter out of shells, knee-deep in the swamp and facing the charging crocodile. The Harbourmaster, seeking Divine guidance, throws his hands in the air. 'ZUT!' he cries passionately.

Of course, the whole aim in going foreign is to dine ashore and soak up atmosphere, preferably at a little place recommended by somebody where only the local fishermen eat. As our party enters, the roar of conversation stops abruptly. Father is suddenly conscious of the jungle-hued brilliance of

the leisure wear knickers he is wearing and of the munching, wooden scrutiny of large men in blue denims and berets. 'Bon er noir er monsieurs,' he greets experimentally. The silence is of the type experienced by archaeologists opening up a long undiscovered tomb. Our party settles down to demolish a stack of washleather crêpes and red anti-freeze as if trying to set up a new record. Madame with the Clark Gable moustache produces *l'addition*, which to her astonished gratification goes unchallenged.

There is an extraordinary belief that going foreign is in some way beneficial to small children, broadening their outlook and embracing as it does new languages, customs and viewpoints. The child's first indication that they are drawing closer to foreign soil may well be a nocturnal ding-dong between dad and mum, carried on above the tumult of wind and wave. '*Where* for God's sake?' demands Daddy. Mummy's voice tweets in the background. 'It's no use just telling me you can see a little light going winkety wink,' roars dad, '*Time* the bloody thing, TIME IT.'

The hard truth of the matter is that kids live inside a personal blister pack of habit, sustained on fish fingers and chips, and the hell with your squid cooked in its own ink. For their entertainment, kids require sand, be it coral, volcanic or Blackpool. Your sneering flamenco dancer may be stamping around in musical fury, as if something horrid was stuck to his boot, and from a'top the slender minaret may come the tremulous wail of the muezzin, understandable in view of his precarious and dizzy perch, but nothing registers in the gyro-compass controlled mind of a child. 'But you promised us a beach . . .' they accuse, dodging the flying fish.

Many folk keep their boats afloat until after Christmas, after which an English winter becomes utterly disgusting. East Coast yachtsmen in particular favour this form of fleshly mortification. Why hog it in an armchair by the fire, they sneer, when you might be filling your lungs with ozone, cheeks rosy, eyes a'sparkle at the sting o' the flying spray. Who wants to be a couch potato eh? They challenge. Well I bloody do for one mate.

The reality is that you'll spend two or three miserable hours lurching over leaden seas under a louring sky with dead fingers and marble toes inside so many pairs of socks that you totter around like a Chinese lily-foot. Your cheeks are the colour of low-fat milk. When at last (for God's sake) the engine is started, people huddle on the engine box like day-old chicks on an incubator.

It was on one such little exercise that I met Sarah age five. We three grown-ups stayed in the cockpit pretending to fill our grateful lungs with permafrost while Sarah, practically spherical with multiple layers of wool, stayed at the foot of the companionway looking up.

I looked down at her dear little face, so small, so trusting, so vulnerable. I thought; here I stand, driving the ship through this winter's murk and to her I suppose I look big, strong and manly ... a face a child can trust to bring her safely home. Her big round eyes watched me unblinkingly. Have no fear my little one, I thought, flashing her my old Cary Grant smile.

Sarah stretched out her arm, pointing at me. 'That man,' she informed all and sundry accusingly, '... that man has purple ears!'

Staying Out Late

Extending the sailing season should be a carefully planned exercise and not a matter of 'hanging it out a bit', like the last dinner guest, ensconced on the settee, lost in cognac-powered rhetoric, while a tight-lipped and dressing-gowned host is booting the cat out.

In fact, there is nothing better calculated to ruin an insurance underwriter's day than the news that a yacht, hitherto assumed to be safely propped up in the lee of a shed with her engine full of anti-freeze, is in reality being towed home astern of a crabber whose skipper is smacking his lips and punching his calculator.

Yet more often than not, the decision to stay afloat a bit longer is a hasty one, inspired by a lousy summer and freaky October sunshine. 'I think I'll stay out a bit longer,' says father, implying a night with the lads and a songful return at dawn. Preparation is vital. Just as an explorer about to plunge into primeval jungle should have a thorough medical beforehand, a proper strip-off, complete with specimen and a bath the night before ('And you're not wearing those, Norman!') so also must a yacht have a check of equal thoroughness.

A squirt of oil in the jib roller, a quick glance at the masthead via the binos and the discovery of a sprouting onion in a hanging locker does not constitute adequate preparation for what is to come.

The popular concept of a winter sail is of a keen, clean wind drawn deeply and beneficially into the lungs, with a shudder of sheer gratitude, while cheeks are apple-red, eyes sparkle and the sea glitters whitely in winter sunshine. Father surveys the empty seascape with satisfaction. 'By God, other people just don't know what they are missing!' he sneers. What *he* has missed is the last weather bulletin. Below decks the bulkhead barometer hand is unwinding like a test-your-grip machine, smacks are hurrying for shelter and seagulls are flogging inland with grim intent.

The truth about winter sailing is somewhat different. Crew crouch in the lee of the dodger or roost on the top step of the companionway, where some faint and frowsty warmth may be rising. Dead fingers, like oven-ready chips, grip mugs of Bovril into which mottled purple noses drip rhythmically. A shapeless woollen hummock is steering and Father, exhibiting a new and novel dedication to the navigator's ancient art, works away snugly down below.

On arrival he emerges to survey an empty and rainswept anchorage with the pride of a conjurer producing doves from a top hat. 'We've got the pick of the berths,' he proclaims to his silent and shuddering crew. With an unerring ineptitude perfected over years of nautical cock-ups, he selects a mooring which is two years overdue for replacement and has about as much tensile strength as a suspender belt. 'I'll be very surprised if anyone comes back and claims this,' he laughs in an uncanny show of clairvoyance.

The ideal winter weekend involves a short and rugged sail to a sheltered anchorage, and thereafter a cosy evening below yarning under the cabin lamp. There follows the sweet benison of deep and dreamless slumber, then hey-ho sizzling bacon on a crisp bright morning and a free wind home again. Ideal, also, would be a video user's manual written by Enid Blyton. We know those jolly evenings. The saloon will be about as cosy as a haunted crypt. Monkish figures wearing sleeping bags play a few hands of Newmarket. Then, secretly vowing 'Never again!', they turn in to lie curled in the foetal position in a vain attempt to bring frozen feet into the meagre warmth of the pelvic region.

Much depends on what sort of cabin heater you've got; whether a fan wafts diesel fumes up your hooter or a bulkhead-mounted catalytic heater envelops your head in wet fug while your socks crackle with frost.

Old Harry suffers none of these ills. His great pot-bellied bogey stove crouches on bandy iron legs like some wild beast poised ready to spring. The stranger would feel an urge to approach cracking a whip and brandishing a chair. The application of a match triggers a dramatic transformation.

With the stack pipe rumbling like Mount Etna and clouds of paraffin and coke fumes rolling over grateful crews moored downwind, he can work up a fug like a polecat's den inside half an hour. From every crack and knothole in the cabin sole cold air comes whistling in to replace the carbon monoxide. You could play the foot locker finger-holes like a piccolo.

Shucked down to long-johns, slippers and cap, Old Harry makes regular trips deck-side to replenish the water in the deck fitting, which serves the valuable function of cooling the chimney and preventing the deck from bursting into flame. A refugee column of cockroaches files aloft, routed by a choking miasma of coke, Robin Redbreast Flake and drying socks.

Those days are long gone. Winter evenings below are endless when sunset is at 1600. No lazy drinks and salted nuts in the cockpit, watching the howling incompetence of fellow yachtsmen berthing down-wind. Instead, you sit huddled over your Scrabble tiles in the yellow 5W glimmer. Aloft a halyard raps. 'OOOOOooooOOOOO' sorrows the wind generator. The bulkhead heater creates a reptile house fug from the waist upwards. It is time for relaxation and the witty cut and thrust of conversation.

'For God's sake, Howard, it's only a game!' grits Mother, rolling an exasperated eye upwards to the condensation-streaming skylight. Father is stuck with letter 'q' again. The bag wasn't shaken properly he complains. 'Qak' he tries hopefully. There is a howl of wind and the boat slams back on her chain. 'Qup?' he offers, without much conviction. The evening stretches ahead and, 'Why goodness me, it's five o'clock already.'

Then there is passage-making. In June it is hardly dark

before dawn is flinging silver darts among the paling stars and laughing fellow watch-mates swap anecdotes as their frail barque curtsies on her way. (Note: Percy, who lacks both chin and assertiveness, never gets beyond, 'I remember when ...')

By contrast, a winter passage at night drags on like a finance committee meeting held in a public urinal. In the days of the coke bogie smouldering cheerfully below, it was, admittedly, different. Then your helmsman could sit back and savour deep breaths of paraffin sidelight, stove fumes and, from the companionway, a cocktail of wet wool, horse-hair, rotting linoleum, bilge, bacon, bucket, dry rot and socks steaming over the bogie.

Dressing for a winter sail can make the cash tills tinkle like merry sleigh bells. Crews blunder around lagged like bath-room boilers in multiple layers of padding, which render a simple call of nature a bitter struggle ... like hunting for a lost ferret. 'Laugh at winter's chills,' urge the advertisements, hinting at near hysterical matrons helpless with mirth in vast fleecy bloomers. The hidden snag lies in the thermal under-wear which has to be donned in private and prior to embarkation. The total novice invited for a day's sail and investing in such garments will be treated to a car ride to the marina with the heating going full blast. Already beginning to glow, the day turns out to be unseasonably warm; there will be sunbathers in Hyde Park. Ashore again, and brewing up nicely, there is the drive home and 'Let's drop in on old Sid and Mabel', souls of centrally-heated hospitality.

The only hope of avoiding spontaneous combustion is a furtive trip to the bathroom and a rapid strip-off. Our host, a keen first-aider, alerted by the sweat-streaked and crimson complexion, listens knowledgeably to the bumps and grunts from within. 'He may be swallowing his tongue,' he warns disturbingly, hurling a sturdy shoulder against the door.

Major amongst a dazzling selection of discomforts is cold feet. The traditional remedy was for a helmsman thus afflicted to sit with a lighted paraffin lamp between his feet and a sailbag over all – a risky stratagem which has been known to trigger a helmsman into an abrupt and howling dash for the rail terminating in a splash and a sizzle. On frosty nights also, the wearing of a sleeping bag while on watch was not unknown; a favourite ruse of the 50s and giving rise in times of sudden emergency to a cockpit full of bounding figures like huge jumping beans.

But if evenings are endless, the mornings are of stunning nastiness. Crews awake to an atmosphere like the inside of a wet rubber glove. Wary eyes open and snap shut again, like mussels. The ready-filled kettle stands on the cooker, but who will get up and light it? Typically it will be the owner, master-under-God and keeper of the cheque book, who finally emerges and shuffling in his sleeping bag like some nightmare grub, lights it and retires to his pit. He has lit the gas, but who will make the tea? It will take three hours to get the ship under way. Three hours of silence, broken only by shudders and grunts. There is only one mercy. There are no women aboard so nobody has to wash.

t is going public the very first time that terrifies us. You have had your test run up the garden and back; no curtains flickered. She says, 'You can roll up the cuffs can't you and it'll probably run up a little first time its washed.' Has it some sinister life of its own then?

So you take one tuck in. It comes right down to your thighs. You feel like a bloody caterpillar. On the way to the club you pause to study the reflection in a shop window, a pace this way a pace that, then you note the display of surgical goods. 'Oh good afternoon Mrs Ponsonby.'

The barman knows his place. Not for the likes o' him to pass remarks about the gennalum members. He winces when you hit him with the full glory of maroon and green vertical stripes. Your fingertips emerge from the cuff like some creature emerging from its lair and close around the mug handle. 'All the best and have one yourself Joe.' Joe would be pleased to have one. He draws off a half-pint without shifting his entranced gaze from your tropical brilliance. It fills his left boot.

Wool and the Wobbling Sternum

he concept of displaying commercial advertising on one's chest, or exhortations to ban this or save that has no historical precedent. Ban the Gatling Gun; Save the Dodo; Virol for growing girls; Iron Jelloids? Chests were plain, apart from those of paid hands, labelled with their yacht's name for rapid identification when stowed in some reeking forepeak among the sailbags.

To see the traditional gansy at its best we must turn to Old Harry's wardrobe – a somewhat fanciful description for the row of nails behind the door to the forepeak. Once donned, his gansy becomes a permanency – a woollen carapace reinforced by a heavy patina of porridge and sump oil, varnish, antifouling and best bitter. It has the resonance of a bodran when drummed upon with a spoon and it is impervious to water and attack by termite or moth.

There were the ancient traditional patterns knitted by keening women in the light of tallow dips, symbolic and concerned with dire and watery fates, but they were a far cry from Doreen with her wobbling art gallery – a chest of such pneumatic magnificence that it might have been better employed in the raising of historic wrecks from the seabed.

The convention of wearing a pictorial anchor athwart one's sternum sticks resolutely to the traditional fisherman pattern, fouled by a bit of left-handed rope. Meon, CQR, or similar burying types might prove more efficacious, although, in view of the nature of the holding ground, on occasions the addition of a tripping line and buoy might be advisable.

Knitting a sweater for a yachtsman is about as rewarding as papering the boy's bedroom with Canalettos. It starts with those patterns in women's mags. 'Ahoy there!' they announce. 'Be shipmates with this hunky, chunky-knit sweater for the him in your life.'

A picture shows a young man lagged to the glottis in Fair Isle and wearing a taut expression – as well he might, seeing the picture was taken in the office with the heating full on.

'Just the thing for your birthday,' says Nora, donning the black cap. 'Would you like it in yellow, beige or smoky green?' He wants it in navy, grey or speckled – the latter colour having the virtue of being wearable for six months at a time before it sees the washtub, when it renders more alluvial silt than the Nile Delta. The knitting pattern presumes a recipient with broad shoulders and narrow hips. Norman is the other way round. He winds up looking like a traffic cone in chainmail.

A hand-knitted sweater is highly labour-intensive and as vulnerable to damage as a matchstick model of the Sydney Opera House left on a sofa. To wear such a garment at fitting-out time suggests the sheer bravado of bullfighting on a unicycle. A *white* hand-knitted sweater is sensitive to brown Windsor soup at twenty paces. There are bitter expatriates living in Patagonia who never went home after a day spent smacking on anti-fouling while wearing a birth-day sweater.

The owner of such a sweater will already have suffered the period of its gestation. He gets to know when she is 'casting on' and tip-toes around the house as if a sickroom crisis was brewing. One ill-timed word and she will lose count – a cata-strophe on a par with shouting 'Boo' to a keyhole surgeon.

He learns when she desires to wind wool and to proffer his wrists as if in an act of surrender. Or he will rise in mid-sports page and extend both arms in the manner of Moses delivering a prophecy while she offers up the embryo garment for measurement – a ritual which will do little to guarantee a fit. The pattern, she will tell him, is for a normal figure.

Once the garment is complete, Norman begins to endure a life of tyranny. 'You're surely not thinking of doing that in your nice sweater!' she honks. Or if he doesn't wear it … 'You never seem to wear your nice sweater these days.'

He will be exhibited to women friends, rotating obediently. It has a particularly interesting (traditional) pattern which consists of a line of great buboes across the chest, like some obscure tropical plague. Myopic immunologists call for immediate isolation. It looks like a relief map of the Kyles of Bute and uses another two sheep's-worth of wool.

Being the owner of a little masterpiece, Whistler's Mother on No 6 needles, is no easy role and he longs for his old navy rollneck, with the sleeves shattered as though a shotgun had

been discharged down each, ex-Millets and long-since vanished from his drawer. He suspects the church jumble. With its creator constantly circling him, flicking and tugging at collar and hem, endlessly adjusting like a live steam buff with cotton waste and oil can ministering to a traction engine, he gets little respite.

The fact that the wind goes straight through it like a garden trellis makes no difference. To attempt any manoeuvre, beyond standing stock still, is akin to donning the Coronation Regalia to whitewash the outside toilet. Her eye never leaves it, running over it as though carrying out a pre-flight check. Michelangelo probably eyed the roof of the Sistine Chapel for bat-droppings with the same critical scrutiny. The first time she washes it is major surgery. Thereafter, it spends days in convalescence, spreadeagled on a towel, tugged this way and that in a ritual post-operative care designed to restore its original unaccommodating shape.

The man who attempts to wash his own sweater needs to be fearless and of philosophical resignation. OK, so it was only one sleeve that brushed the fly-wheel, only one bit of Branston pickle on the sternum, but to wash it himself is a hanging offence. The washing machine yields up either a woollen octopus or a felt toy that might fit dolly.

When is the next flight to Tierra del Fuego?

Any sort of drying out is fraught with peril.

The owner of a twin-keel cruiser on a drying out mud mooring has a prime hate – the bait-digger. Armed with fork and bait-box and wearing a cloth cap, a dog-end stuck to his lower lip and a permanent drip on his nose, your bait-digger leaves in his plodding wake a No-man's Land of craters. Add some barbed wire and a few poppies and you have a ready-made film set for Journey's End. It is these craters that cause the aggro.

Your thigh booted owner wading out to his boat on the first trickle of flood tide makes a fine and manly picture. He is carrying oars, rowlocks, sailbags, a packed lunch and Doreen. This is to be her first sail, or to coin an unhappy phrase, she is about to, er, take the plunge. He sticks his great boot into this bait-hole ...

Or, afloat and about to anchor over a nice flat stretch of foreshore upon which he will later dry out to stand comfortably upright on his keels, he pokes around with his boathook. He does not discover the yawning abyss beneath his starboard keel. 'We'll be able to walk ashore later on,' he promises, 'if we feel inclined,' he concludes with uncanny clairvoyance.

She Ought to Have a Leg Out

'I think we may have to dry out,' says Father, implying some gloomy regime of carrot juice, beanshoots and press-ups under the flinty eye of a Swedish masseuse. He surveys the suspiciously empty berths alongside the quay with the innocence of Little Red Riding Hood sampling porridge. Apart from one battered vessel strewn with window-boxes, tomato Gro-Bags and a hoodless perambulator, he has a free choice.

'At least it will be easier to take on fresh water,' he notes prophetically, lying alongside directly under the town storm drain. As if on cue, thunder clouds begin massing on the horizon.

To the novice, drying out alongside is an uneasy balancing act rendered no simpler by the instructions outlined in books and magazine articles, which imply something between pole squatting and levitation. Cocooned to the wall by a mesh of ropes, our Master watches the slow exposure of slimy seawall, like a condemned man watching the sunrise. Mussels slam shut their shutters like post office clerks whose queues have achieved record lengths. The yacht dries out exactly and horrifyingly upright.

Setting the correct angle of heel calls for a steady eye. Holding aloft a ring spanner on a length of string, Father walks steadily backwards along the edge of the quay, sighting against the angle of the mast. 'Pardon me for arstin' squire ...' interrupts a holidaymaker in a cardboard yachting cap and a Union Jack vest, 'but ...'

'I am about to dry out,' snaps Father impatiently and, as it happens, untruthfully. He trips over a ringbolt and vanishes with a falsetto howl. There is a tremendous splash.

'*Once lines and trim are correctly adjusted ...*' we yachting writers prattle, berthed safely alongside our desks, '... *the vessel should see herself down without further need for attention.*'

We close our minds resolutely to the mental picture of a crew returning from a long hot day of sightseeing to find an ominous gap at the quayside, spectators peering downwards and a fire pump chattering nearby.

There are two distinct schools of thought on the matter of heeling the ship to lie against a wall: the induced list and the masthead rope. The latter, it must be said, is a pitfall for the forgetful, for whom it is like having a drink in one hand, a cocktail canapé in the other and no recollection whatsoever of having done up his zip. Masthead rope advocates are a familiar sight in waterside restaurants. They have forgotten to ease it off. Smiles snap off, they jerk upright with popping eye and a fragment of Crêpe Suzette falls from tremulous lips like an autumn leaf.

'*A dinghy partly filled with water on the sidedeck provides a simple form of trimming ballast ...*' rattle the yachting writers happily. It is not a stratagem always viewed with pleasure by returning late-night revellers.

'Jump Sandra, I've got you,' laughs Father, with amorous gallantry, too drunk to detect the difference between well-filled designer jeans and Norman's sensible serge. Sandra, breathing raw Calvados fit to power a hot-air balloon, launches herself into space.

It is perhaps fortunate that few readers accept our dictums with simple and childlike faith, preferring to line the inboard side as if queuing for free soup. Other concessions to trim can prove more disturbing. Father fiddles around under the saloon table, which collapses with a crash, metamorphosing as a double bed.

'I think you'd better come in with me on my side tonight, Mildred,' he announces. She simpers and flutters girlishly, tactics which cost him his bachelor status 30 years earlier. 'We'll have all your weight where it will do most good.' Mildred begins banging pans around in the galley.

Old Harry dries out with the regularity of supper-in-the-oven on yoga nights. It is a recurring misfortune ascribable to the abolition of the fathom from charts and the substitution of 'metric water' – an unsatisfactory foreign fluid and faintly frivolous like French mustard.

To your ordinary owner, life at an angle places a severe strain upon the matrimonial bond. '... even a fool could have seen that we were out of the channel!' Tight-lipped Father pours gin at an angle of 35° into a glass held at 40° and fills her left Docksider.

Old Harry, on the other hand, seizes the opportunity to inspect his garboards, tingle his stem-hook and rouse out the gribble and other watery residents of his rudder trunk.

Antifouling brush in hand he lays about the mighty haunches of his converted winkle shoveller, pausing only as the flood tide begins trickling past. A broad swathe of this lethal nostrum is borne swiftly through the anchorage, adding a gay note of colour to the waterlines of the assembled fleet.

When in harbour it is usually the women who take over full command, a domestic arrangement which has the Master-under-God shuttling between ship and shops lugging gas bottles, huge economy-sized everything and over-ripe tomatoes which 'any fool with eyes in his head should have spotted'.

But in a drying berth her authority counts for naught. 'I'll have to stay aboard and see her down, dear,' he raps crisply. He watches her out of sight through the loo porthole then settles back full-length on the settee to wait, dribbling on her scatter cushions, making up for lost sleep and a night spent, stopwatch in hand, timing car headlights three-every-ten as they passed a gap in a distant hedge. Meanwhile, and like a cat having kittens, the yacht grounds herself privately and without fuss.

It cannot be denied that berthing alongside and drying out can cause serious family rifts, witness that distressing business with cousin Mabel. Invited along, following her operation for you-know-what and in the correct expectation that the sea air would put some colour in her cheeks (it did, green), she was on the next plane home an hour after the keel hit the sea-bed.

A confirmed secret All-Bran eater, her discovery that the toilet compartment had the acoustical properties of Ely Cathedral made Mabel understandably furtive about her visits, and the sudden and mysterious exodus of all hands on deck was a chance not to be missed.

'Where's Mabel?' demanded Father after a head count.

'In the lavvy, in the lavvy!' chorused the twins, thereby and unwittingly deleting their names from her last-will-and-testament. With gritted teeth, Mabel sat it out like a cornered rat in a bread bin, despite all injunctions to 'do that later, sit

well inboard and make no sudden movements' (unlikely in the event). Her taxi driver to the airport stood examining his tip as though it might be of numismatic rarity.

The actual moment of taking the ground is the crux of the whole thing, and no matter how thorough the preparations, the unexpected can never be ruled out.

An owner may have such vast experience that his cap badge is in the final stages of electrolytic disintegration, but he can still be caught out like any novice. He has adjusted lines and fenders to perfection, the angle of heel is precise. The ebb is away, below his keel crabs glance up apprehensively. 'I think we can look forward to a quiet night,' he forecasts with disastrous naïvety; he is in a fishing boat berth. Approaching the harbour entrance is a Breton crabber: her bow-wave is level with the top of her wheelhouse, her skipper is black of visage, late for his boules match and has a lousy catch.

Turning in, while aware that the ship will be setting herself on, calls for nerves of steel and the faintest creak of warp or fender triggers Father out of his pit like a partridge startled by the sportsman's fateful tread, which is why he elects to take the unselfish course of watching her down. 'You lot get your heads down,' he offers generously. Thereafter, he will be busy as a clockwork hen, up and down the steps, rattling the rigging, thumping the anchor around on the sidedeck, sighing, yawning, humming and clattering in the galley, while the crew, ungrateful recipients of his unselfishness, lie wakeful and cursing. Or he may while away the time by sorting the chart table drawer, tut-tutting at his discoveries. This may be followed by a length and detailed study of the nautical almanac, from which he learns that *antiseekrankheitsmittel* is German for seasick pill and that a collection of old newspaper can be valuable in cases of emergency childbirth.

He wakes with a snort an hour later to find the ship hard on. Next time it will be an alarm clock job with the entire crew jerked awake, babbling their mothers' names and performing running or swimming motions according to the nature and novelty of individual nightmares.

The wives of skippers addicted to drying out come to dread what they term 'fuss and performance' and what Father calls 'acting in a proper and seamanlike manner'.

'Oh, you may think I fuss a bit,' he smiles, raising the hand of reasonability. He pauses to allow time for a general denial. The saloon clock ticks loudly in the silence. 'Now that she's on, you can hop around to your heart's content,' he adds, implying some sort of jollity involving concertina and fiddle.

At this moment a salvage tug comes belting down harbour *en route* for some lucrative navigational cock-up on an offshore bank. She is pulling a wake like the Severn Bore in full spate, which lifts the yacht and slams her down with a crash 2ft further out, where she sticks immovable as a pig on a front lawn.

There follows total chaos with the ebb dropping at dizzy speed. All hands turn to stuffing anything and everything between ship and wall. 'Not my scatter ...' wails Mother belatedly. There is a scrunch. 'Guardrails, guardrails!' howls Father. From aloft there comes a deep and vibrant humming, like bees amongst the hollyhocks. 'Cap shrouds, cap shrouds!' he pipes, frantically unwinding a bottlescrew. It is a long, long wait for the returning flood that day and Father never stirs from the forepeak, while onlookers feast their eyes and suck their teeth in happy disapproval.

While the techniques should never be discussed in public and out of context ('Does she lie with her head down? If I'm going to put her against the wall, I like her to have a leg out ...' etc), a yacht in this curious state has a magnetic attraction for onlookers.

Peering down, they watch silently and intently, like medical students observing a lobectomy or, to use a more graphic simile, like the lifting of a flat stone to reveal the fascinating and busy life of an ant's nest, as the creatures rush hither and thither with their eggs – an exercise mirrored by Mother with her scatter cushions.

The spellbound onlookers can progress slowly from a view down the companionway to the busy doings visible via the saloon skylight and finally, as a sort of grande finale, to the open forehatch, beneath which Norman, in the sad belief that he is enjoying total privacy behind locked doors, is applying The Ointment as instructed, three times daily and to affected areas.

Drying out is not a procedure to employ unless all members of the crew are full-blown sailors, and hairy-chested with it, particularly in areas of great tidal range. Here, the party is preparing to dine ashore.

'Mightn't slacks have been better my love?' wheedles Father, eyeing her white pleated skirt with sinking heart and gloomy clairvoyance. Knowing full well what awaits their return three hours hence and at low tide, he would like to recommend a boilersuit, boots, hard hat and industrial mitts, but it seems that he is denying her the one chance she has of wearing the few miserable rags she managed to pack, and does he expect *everybody* to go round looking like a tramp? He volunteers to stay on board and rig bosun's chairs.

Three hours and four bottles of the house red later, the party returns. The crosstrees are at foot level and the route back aboard is via a rusty, oily and vertical iron ladder vanishing into a black void, thence a crotch-wrenching backwards step feeling for a broomstick lashed athwart the shrouds.

The greenish sodium lighting of the quayside illuminates the upturned faces and reaching hands of those already down on deck, giving an eerie impression of the souls of the damned on Judgement Day. Later for Father, in the privacy of the forecabin and in hissing undertones, Judgement Day is precisely what it turns out to be.

The fact that it is lady-wife who does the cooking in ninety per-cent of small family cruisers is not the blatant example of sexism it might appear. Any woman who has suffered that rare treat, breakfast in bed, would rather drag herself cookerwards with chin ploughing a furrow through the shag-pile than experience another. Toast shatters into blackened shards like newly unearthed grave-goods the moment an attempt is made to butter it. A fried egg clatters as it hits the plate, bacon disintegrates like some fragmentation grenade and the beans, oh yes beans too, have the texture of a leather bookmark. Then comes clearing up after him. The galley looks like a national emergency. All it lacks is the TV cameras and a distribution of free soup.

Porridge on the Deckhead

The design convention that places the galley alongside engine and chart table is much akin to sticking a toxic waste disposal unit and a coal-fired power station next door to Greenpeace Head Office.

'Just try to tell the court in your own words how it was that your wife came to hit you with the frying pan,' coaxes the magistrate gently.

'All I did was to have a look at my little dipstick and whammy,' croaks the plaintiff brokenly.

Men are mostly to blame. Old dad gets the urge to work up a passage plan and check oil and battery the very moment that Norma starts banging pans around. Up come the floorboards and the engine box lid, and just let her put a packet of Wunda-soop on his chart table and the violins begin to play.

'Please, *not* on my chart table,' he whines, spreading a protective arm. 'Anywhere else (like where for pity's sake?) but *not on the chart table!*'

She clamps her lips tight and clatters. Bang goes the pan of steaming spuds on the bottom step of the companionway ladder. Squelch goes Percy's non-slip straight in it and off he speeds with a howl. Clank-thud, clank-thud, clank.

In most well-dominated cruisers where the galley working area is athwart the companionway, a man needs the foot-work of a Highland dancer if he isn't to be trapped below when cooking begins. Getting to the ladder is like trying to beat the Edinburgh Express to a level crossing. Apologies get you nowhere.

'Sorry, if I might just *squeeze* by,' smirks old dad nervously. A blue denim rump jerks out with the speed of a striking cobra barring his path and her lips smack shut like a neo-prene clack-valve. It is at this point that your wise man, anxious to forestall the old shuddering sigh routine, turns back and uses the forehatch. You may *think* she's busy rum-maging in a locker and that the way is clear, but just you try it, mate, that's all. Like a World Cup goalie she bounds back and saves your shot before you can get a toe on the first step.

It is not easy to aspire to gracious living in the modern go-go cruiser. Cooking while going to windward is like trying to stand in a deckchair to paper the ceiling. At intervals of roughly ten waves, the cook, wearing a toupee of Spanish omelette, raises wan and haggard features from the hatch, gulps and is thrust back down again by firm but kindly hands.

'Dining out' takes on a new and terrible significance far removed from the kiss of candlelight on soft, bare shoulder. ('I do wish you'd wear a suit sometimes, Gerald.')

At sea nobody goes below unless for the basic necessities of sleep, defecation and navigation – which accounts, on occasion, for some new and novel landfalls. They sit up there to windward stuffing nourishment into the depths of their hoods, crumbs streaming to leeward, Percy at his customary leerail position, staring at a hunk of veal-and-egg pie like some geologist glumly cataloguing a fossil. Your gourmet, who will engage a *maitre d'* in bitter complaint over the *bouquet garni* in his navarin of lamb, can be found ramming bacon butty into his chops as if packing a suitcase with a taxi at the front door. Your digestive biscuit freaks, grateful for the current of warm air rising from below, huddle around the companionway like terriers round a rat-hole.

Force 6 is boiled egg time. This delicacy o' the deep, the cook's *tour de force*, the product of two high-speed, tight-lipped visits below is whacked down in a big saucepan. Father, never an assertive man ('you let them walk all over you Norman') reaches automatically for the cracked one. 'No, not that one!' commands lady-wife. 'There's a *worse* one than that!'

You'll find the Good Samaritan who'll make some attempt at cooking, who will spend 40 minutes while plunging to windward in Force 7 trying to make porridge for all. He will be running a bit thin on patience. His struggles are noted by the occupants of the saloon berths with the clinical detachment of medical students viewing a hip replacement. 'Well,' he rasps, combing porridge off the deckhead and smacking it back in the pan, 'Who's first?'

A bottom-bunker raises a pallid finger. 'I'll have corn-flakes, if you don't mind,' he wimps.

Most dining afloat takes place in harbour in the dining alcove and around the regulation collapsible table, which has produced a generation of yachtsmen with flattened fingertips. 'We can get five on the inside,' pipes Father, taking damn good care not to be one of them.

Percy, who would rather be up on deck with his Ryvita, is immovably corralled as if about to be branded and - de-horned. He wishes he'd gone easier on the best bitter.

An unpunctured tinned duff remains the major threat.

'I'm sorry, Sir, but the pontoon is closed,' says a policeman, barring the way with upraised palm. 'We've got a tinned pudding alert on. Apple and rhubarb with added fruit flavourings,' he adds grimly.

There is just one hope in such a situation; somebody, scorning personal safety, must nip aboard and turn the gas off. 'I'll ... I'll go, Father,' says young Rodney, his finely chiselled young features working convulsively.

Father raises a gnarled hand. 'Nay lad, nay. You have your whole young life before you. This is a job for an older man. Go get your grandad, son.'

By now the pudding is about to go critical, the rigging is thrumming and from the galley ventilator there comes an angry chattering sound. A fireman hurries by. 'Huff hoff huh hong' he raps urgently through his breathing apparatus. Then comes a tremendous roar. The ventilator goes into orbit and windows shatter; a plug of pudding kills a crow over Leicester.

Provisioning abroad is regarded as a special treat by Brits. 'We don't get bread like this at home,' proclaims lady-wife, thumping a rock-hard baguette on the counter. A cockroach hurries off in overdrive. Father, plagued by the possession of an upper denture that rattles and clacks like an African xylophone, sighs and resigns himself to sucking it like a teething ring.

'Let's see if we can find something fresh,' Norma cries, heading for a morning market that closed an hour ago. She would stand a better chance heading for the catacombs. She is wearing her EU let's-be-Europeans-together smile which, combined with the pursed lips considered essential to the pronunciation of foreign languages (Neanderthal grunts at the check-out) gives her the appearance of a milk jug. There follows Father in his new, stiff, genuine Breton canvas smock, like a walking deckchair, and Percy in his new genuine fisherman's beret; six foot of rippling rib-cage and elbow topped by a beret, spherical in its newness. All too appropriately, he has the appearance of an exclamation mark.

But there can be few exponents of simple healthy fare to equal that arch traditionalist and doyen of the offal counter, Old Harry.

'There's nothing to beat a nice bit o' boiled pork on a night watch,' he claims, grasping your lapels in friendly fashion and rocking you to and fro by way of emphasis. 'Why, you can feel it a'lying here a'nourishing you all night,' he asserts, indicating the precise spot with a bandaged and red-lead dappled finger.

Having the digestive system of a sink disposal unit, he has an unending search for crew. Those hardy or ill-advised enough to ship with him are speedily educated. The watch below, lying with unobstructed view of the galley, stare in dread fascination as he pokes around in a steaming pan.

'Now, this has a bit o' body in it,' he states with accuracy. He holds up a bit of body for their horrified inspection, a great gobbet of fatty tissue that judders and shudders on his fork as if convulsed by some dreadful private joke.

With hands clamped to mouths they quit their bunks as though answering a maroon. Up the ladder they clatter. 'Hold theeth pleeth,' mumbles a sufferer smacking his snappers into the helmsman's hand. He sits studying them, as though assessing the value of some grisly gratuity.

Old Harry, a cook of some standing – eg some standing, but more typically lying and jack-knifing – wastes little by way of ingredients. Apart from hoof and horn, he considers no product of the butcher's block inedible and is particularly partial to a nice sheep's head, 'with the eyes left in so's it will see him through the week,' as he never tires of joking.

Having purchased one with the intention of making a nice drop o' beef tea, he left this revolting tidbit on the end of his bunk, pending return from the Dog and Gooseneck, where the Harbourmaster accosted him for dues.

'I thought I might kitch you here,' apologised this official, 'on account of you not bein' aboard. I had a little look through your scuttle and I seed your lady wife havin' a bit of a lay down ...'

The Annual Club Dinner and Dance

have only worn evening dress once. I collected it from Moss Bros after work and went straight to the Café Royal where I was to pick up my wife – an unhappy turn of phrase, suggesting a quick fireman's lift and an assault on the swing doors. Thus I had no chance for a dummy-run in the bathroom at home and a turn-round-get-your-stomach-in wifely inspection.

I was there first and I hurried down to the gents with my large cardboard box. Once locked in, there followed a mighty rustling of tissue paper punctuated by grunts and exclamations, which to a listener outside might have hinted at some gargantuan bowel movement in progress.

I had seen nothing like those garments, and a perfunctory measuring session in the shop had not prepared me. It was that little waistcoat that foxed me. It seemed to have a complexity of strops, guys, swifters and stays which had to be allied to an equal abundance of buttons in strange places. With elbows drumming on the sides of my narrow retreat, muttered oaths and in mounting panic I assembled my attire. By now Joyce would be waiting in the foyer with bag, gloves, corsage and radiating her displeasure. She might have a revolving blue light on her head.

At last I was ready. I flushed the loo ritualistically and stepped forth in sartorial splendour, tails, tie, dicky and patent shoes. I frowned. There was a curious tension between trouser and sternum which inclined me forwards in a sort of olde worlde bow, a courtly stance smacking of the Colonel and Kentucky Fried Chicken.

Joyce daggered me with a single glance. 'Did I realise how long she'd been standing there like a fool? Why was I stooping like that for God's sake?' she hissed, sideways.

'Like what?' I wimped, tinnily, straightening up. TWANG. A button bounded away over the floor watched by curious bystanders. For the rest of that dreadful evening, throughout cocktails, dinner and the disastrous dance which followed, I was kept busy stuffing my dicky front back like some failed conjurer battling with a rebellious dove.

The Annual Club Dinner and Dance

Once a year they come sneaking out of Moss Bros with their cardboard boxes of rented finery. They are bound by a magic spell to return these by noon Monday or see their coaches turn back into pumpkins and themselves reduced instantly to vest, pants and sock suspenders on the 0830 out of Bishops Stortford. It is the occasion of the club Annual Dinner and Dance, prizegiving and raffle, valuable prizes to be won.

That Father owns his own dinner jacket (and trousers) is confirmed by the greenish opalescence of these garments and the rich patina of ancient mulligatawny on the lapels. With it goes the hand-tied bow which droops beneath his chin like a dead mouse in the talons of some nocturnal predator, evidence of manipulation in mounting panic.

Such a tie has an aura of quality, like thick breakfast pottery: only the best for Father, none of your precarious clip-on jobs, stuck like a martin's nest to plastic guttering.

Not to be outdone, his ladywife, Norma, has a hair-do that cost about the same as a decent pair of winches. It will be kept hidden from view pending official unveiling and a Bishop's blessing, and it is about as vulnerable as a carton of cream buns on the City Line at rush hour. Father will be held personally responsible for any wind in excess of Force 2.

On arrival they repair to their cloakrooms where attendants, having baited their saucers with 50p coins, retire to lie in wait with clothes brushes raised. Father, having had a pee he didn't need and been deprived of his coat, wanders back to the lobby. He doesn't know what the hell to do with his hands. He has the shifty air of a man caught in his pyjamas at the front door taking the milk in. The hair-do is finally revealed. It appears to have been inflated with a pump and coated with spun toffee; all it lacks is a sprinkling of cashew nuts. He notes with resignation that she is speaking in her telephone voice, usually reserved for doctors, parsons and bank managers.

The reception room is a scene of elegance and sophistication with the men all trying to drink while keeping their fingernails hidden, and the ladies, their shoulders powdered like sponge cakes, bent upon mingling, leaving a trail of pollinated dinner jackets in their wake. Father is on his second pint and will be up and down all night ... 'and don't say I never warned you.'

Norma leans close and addresses him from the corner of her mouth as though operating an unusually cumbersome ventriloquist's dummy. 'Order a gottle of gine for the gable,' she mumbles without gooving her gips. He trots off to consult the winelist. The prices read like something from *The Guinness Book of Records*.

Elsewhere a solitary new member has fouled up the seating plan by knowing nobody. He drifts from one group to another wearing his cardboard smile and nodding as if taking part in meaningful dialogue. He looks as if he is collecting fares. His aim is to keep the social secretary off his back, thus frustrating a round of meaningless introductions and ending up with the club bore. He ends up with the club bore – an old gentleman with eyebrows like a thatched porch and a shaky right hand that sprinkles gin and tonic like a crop sprayer. The cocktail din is at peak decibels.

'What have you got then ha?' he bellows, sprinkling lavishly. A lady with a backless dress straightens up with a squawk.

'Oh just the varicose veins ...'

'Jolly good, jolly good. Spinnaker?'

'I've only got a little Dabchick.'

'Ha. Nasty. Should see a doctor, old man.'

The menu is well up to its usual standard of mediocrity, starting with prawn cocktail – a wineglass packed with lettuce and gloop with a small pink figure poised on the rim of the glass. Then comes baby duckling *à l'orange*, although its infant status is questionable, and a human equivalent would sport a moustache and carry a briefcase. For sweet, there is a choice of treacle tart (Father gets the old pursed lip and head wag from head office because she is all too familiar with his upper denture) or Pomme Napoleon. 'Ugh, apple crumble,' pipes a clear young voice, hastily shushed. Its owner is on her first grown-up social occasion and wearing her first bra – a fact evidenced by the periodic circling movement of her left elbow.

The service, as they might have said aboard *The Titanic*, is prone to delay. By the time the starter arrives, Father has eaten enough bread sticks to build a fair-size rook's nest. The staff, specially recruited from barn and hedgerow, appears at intervals, a solid wall of women in black and white bursting forth from swing doors, accompanied by a freezing blast of air that has encountered no obstacle to its path this side of Bear Island.

Brandishing their trays like some fearful weapons of war, they circle the cringing diners, laying about them with their serving spoons. It looks like Custer's Last Stand. Diners sit dodging and feinting right and left.

'Gravy?' raps a muscular waitress with a moustache like a dray horse.

'Thank you, but no,' says Father, lifting a cautionary finger. She has already moved on. He sits contemplating a Brown and dripping digit with resignation.

The aim of the seating plan is to break up the Batman-and-Robin pairing of married couples by placing one gentleman between any two ladies, thereby ensuring a pleasant conversational mix. Thus the embroiderer of church hassocks will become the wiser for knowing where to dig for the best lugworms. Men sit racking their brains to think of topics, ladies sit mentally screaming with boredom. On father's left, an old lady dissects her duckling in deep concentration like a pathologist hunting for clues, and his fair companion to the right is shovelling peas as if she'd had a

ton of coal shot down on her doorstep. She is to learn that Everton played rubbish again and that snow would never surprise him.

Club social secretaries responsible for the seating arrangements are haunted by the nightmare prospect of Old Harry's attendance. They are besieged with whispered requests to exclude him from this group or that, a pass-the-parcel procedure that sifts him out from table after table like riddling clinkers.

Wearing an antiquated dinner jacket which is opalescent green with age and which lends him the eerie appearance of a gigantic dung-beetle, he is finally sandwiched between a new member who booked late and Who Knows Nobody and a man of notorious irascibility who – and God-have-mercy – has been omitted from the seating plan in error. He has never been so insulted in his life it seems.

Old Harry, upon whose head insults rain continually like hail on a tin privvy, proceeds to numb him to a state of catatonic docility. He pours out a non-stop monologue on the virtues of Stockholm tar in the treatment of hoof-rot and ship-worm. A peeled prawn falls from the nerveless lips of his captive audience. 'Awww!' he comments sparingly, pushing his plate away.

The meal grinds to an end. Watch-my-lips Norma, across the table, signals her spouse to go easy on the wine and leave some for the toasts – as though hinting at some curious savoury still to come. He begins dribbling it out as though conducting a litmus test. It is too late. There is a rumble of chairs as diners are called to their feet.

'The Queen, God blesh her,' chorus sixty owlish husbands, sucking air from long-empty glasses.

'Would sir care for a brandy or a liqueur?' wonders a waiter. Father consults head office again, gets the wag, but orders anyway and buys himself a monstrous cigar to boot. There he sits wreathed in smoke, cigar jutting from huge crimson face like a Brixham Trawler in a gale. All he lacks is a wailing woman – which he will get later on, arriving home, kicking the milk bottles over. It is time for the speeches.

The choice of an after-dinner speaker should be an easy matter with an audience rendered glassy-eyed on bargain Burgundy and sitting beaming and relaxed, ready to guffaw at anything from an auditor's report to a Diocesan Letter. A speaker cannot go far wrong if he makes his entry wobbling along on a unicycle, wearing vast check trousers and juggling eggs.

For club Hon Secs, the task of choosing a speaker should be undertaken as though booking a novelty act, and candidates should be asked to supply a set of 10 x 8 glossies for study. 'There's this one who does the farmyard impressions,' says the Hon Sec, handing the snaps around ... 'or there's this chap who does a bit of magic.' He frowns. 'I'm not sure about the doves though.'

There is a strong element of gamble, like buying a bumper box of Christmas crackers from a street trader. It turns out to have identical hats of minute circumference, whistles that don't blow and riddles in Taiwanese. In our case, a speaker of note has dropped them in it at short notice and mentioned Percy as an available substitute.

Things go wrong for Percy the moment he enters the reception room. He pauses in the doorway waiting for his hosts to spot him. They don't. He feels debonair, suave in his re-cut ex-bankrupt stock dinner jacket. He smiles around with a faintly world-weary, mocking air: the man who has seen it all, done it, been there. A hand tugs his sleeve. 'Two gins, ice, no lemon and a brandy mac please,' demands its owner.

As the meal grinds on, Percy becomes withdrawn. He pats his pocket frequently to make sure that his great wad of notes (it would choke a shredder) is still there. The bathroom eloquence of earlier deserts him like rats leaving a sinking ship. He has armed himself with A Joke, as might some researcher into the occult memorise an incantation of proven efficacy against the powers of evil. It is just about as funny.

On the advice of a well-wisher he has also equipped himself with a tranquilliser pill. He reasons that it must be taken neither too early nor too late. Midway through the sweet course should be about right; he can palm it into his mouth by faking a little cough. The pill is of formidable proportions and if equipped with fins and a warhead, could be of value in submarine warfare. Percy blows it clear across the table. Surprised diners note its bouncing progress with keen interest and it is retrieved from under a nearby table after some shuffling of chairs. A waiter returns it on a plate accompanied by a glass of water. The whole room is now agog, watching the little drama with eyes melting with compassion.

By the time Percy is due to rise, he has been triggered to

his feet like a faulty pop-up toaster twice already by the rap of the gavel, first for the loyal toast and again when the Commodore is due to flap his wattles. His moment arrives. He rises warily and jerkily as if assisted by airbags. He is wearing a square and mirthless grin like a letterbox flap. He swallows hugely. He is encouraged by the warm smiles of his audience, unaware that his tie is hanging by one tiny claw like some bat about to depart upon its nightly foray of terror. He clears his throat.

'Mister Coddlemore ...' he begins, fatally. His ears light up like the Blackpool illuminations.

Once started, and with his sheaf of notes vibrating like a car rally navigator's map, he bleats on and on. His wife sits gritting her teeth, toes curled and napkin balled up to the size of a walnut. It would seem that Percy is delighted to be standing there, which is about as plausible as a condemned man claiming to enjoy the view from the scaffold. The meal, he says, will long be remembered. Then comes The Joke. He should have called his audience to its feet and donned the Black Cap. It goes down like a brick duck. He has loused up the whole thing and missed out the punch line. The audience sits stunned.

'But seriously though ...' Percy flounders on, as if anything could be more serious than his joke, 'It only remains for me to ask my fellow guests to stand and join me in a test to our ghosts.'

There remains the prizegiving (Percy has earlier tapped out his pipe in the Aggregate Points Salver). The last cadet shambles back to his seat with his egg-cup, and the room is cleared for dancing to Viv and his Vampires. A dozen old war-wounds start playing up and their owners limp mightily towards the bar. The Commodore and his lady, who is wearing a gown that makes her look like a hobby horse, take the floor for the opening quickstep.

As guest speaker Percy, aware of his duty, has next round with her. They blunder around, buttocks rigid, glaring fiercely over each other's shoulders as if on the lookout for

whales. It is like steering a loaded supermarket trolley. They end up in a corner, manoeuvring in circles as if waiting for a lock to open.

Then comes the Grand Raffle, when unwanted Christmas presents change owners. The Highland Shortbread Assortment has been going the rounds since Culloden. From now on the floor belongs to the young set wearing weird mauve DJs. Father is content to watch the slit skirts go by. 'My word,' he ho-hos in his avuncular voice, 'That young Perkins girl has shot up, ho ho.' Norma watches him narrowly.

After a tankful of bitter, house red, brandy and more bitter, Father feels at his wittiest, a raconteur and handsome with it. In the mirror of the gents' loo, lit by a strip lamp that could X-ray an ox, he is confronted by a raddled old goat with its bow tie at ten to five, an unbuttoned shirt and a glimpse of greyish Airtex. It is time to go home.

f you work on the staff of a magazine you get to be used as a guinea pig for new products. There was 'Mani-hose' for instance – tights for men. I had a trip to Sweden in mid-winter. 'Ideal,' I told myself. I wished I hadn't listened. I donned it at home at 6 am. I looked like some sort of gargantuan pixie. It was very, very *cosy*.

The train was sizzling hot, and so was Heathrow and the plane, so was the arrival lounge and the host-bus (the trip was a Volvo Penta freebie). I was taken straight to a restaurant like the Matto Grosso, with steam jetting out of both ears and thence to a cabaret. My face was streaming sweat and the colour of a red pepper. 'I tink you feel oil!' said my host with concern. 'Oil?' I said. 'Seek.' 'Sihk?' Then I passed out.

There was also the quilted Canadian underwear. With a lampshade on my head I looked like a Chinese peasant. On a Skaw Race of spectacular misery I put off wearing it until the bone-rattling cold made it impossible to delay longer. It was in a plastic bagful of water under a deck leak. My watchmates stopped shuddering with cold in order to shake with mirth. Watchmates are like that.

Out in a Stiff Sou'wester

ime was when your fully oilskinned mariner was rendered impregnable as Traitor's Gate for the price of a pint of boiled linseed. That was before your state-o-the-art mob stuck its honker in and the cash registers started peep-peeping. It was a sad day when big business cornered our oily trousers ('Ha! kick me would you? Back, back you yellow swine . . .')

No longer will we find old dad kneeling on his foredeck with both ankles gushing water like some miraculous well, no longer does mum sit shuddering in her puddle at the helm dreaming of Benidorm. Nowadays we have the all-everything all-breathing clothing system complete with auto-barometric thermal knickers calling for a second mortgage.

To inspire confidence in the punter any suit of hi-tech protective garments ('oilies' are out) must be a byproduct of either the offshore oil industry or space-walking technology, which makes it ideal for prancing around on the foredeck in a head sea.

Take Gregory, who really believes that buying a certain brand of instant coffee guarantees him a ravishing female neighbour (he gets a cub mistress with a moustache and hips like a tank turret). He buys his foul-weather gear with all the innocence of Christopher Robin out with Nanny, and can't wait to test it out.

'Look folks!' he rejoices, specially designed for Shell .....' Assuming that oil rigs demand buoyancy he steps overboard. Shipmates eye the ascending column of bubbles gloomily. '....... forecourt attendants,' they finish sorrowfully.

Whatever will they think of next, we ask ourselves – a bit pointlessly since nobody's listening. Perhaps we can look forward to the fully waterproof auto-adjusting thermal suit lined with heating/cooling elements and powered by solar panels. The wearer, covered with tiles like an armadillo, emits a continuous humming sound, vibrating as sensors sample body temperature. At irregular intervals he goes into a series of jerks and shudders like a washing machine launching into its final spin.

Already the *thinking* suit is on the way. In the wicked old past, attention to male requirements when dressed for a cold wet night watch was like rummaging in panic through an over-stuffed filing cabinet. Now we have the Musto portcullis system which is unisex and almost automatic. Down rattles the tail-board at the touch of a zip as if delivering furnace nuts down a coalhole.

Breathable fabrics with nine billion pores per square inch let the flavour flood through. Not that this is a new departure. Anyone who has been shipmates with Old Harry and his flannel onepiece Union Suit will know all about breathability – his suit breathes, whilst other people *hold* theirs; an evening down below with him is like sharing a hot lift with a Kurdish goat.

Advertisements for oilies were once of a more restrained nature and women didn't figure at all – a sailor collar and enough buttoned boot to inflame the passions of the boatman were the limit. A steel engraving showed a nautical figure imprisoned in a vast black and multi-buttoned cylinder which reached from ankle to moustachio. It had a double gussetted storm front that would stop a charging rhino and it was topped by a sou'wester like a cricket pavilion. The whole ensemble rendered the wearer immovable beyond a rudimentary shuffle.

Also on offer to Victorian seafarers were the waterproof knee-wrapper and the collapsible rubber bath. What bitter innuendo is contained in that title! Out pops a bung. Seated in a nest of bubbly, soapy rubber, mother-naked, sits our wrathful and bellowing owner.

Today's advertising has technological appeal..., 'Continuous hydrophilic layers evacuate moisture via their molecular structures...' Father nods his approval. He wouldn't recognise a hydrophilic barrier if it bit him in the ankle. He lugs out his chequebook. Anything that keeps him dry and warm at 3 am of a stinking morning has got to be a winner.

Old Harry proves the exception to such seduction. His oilskin coat has a monumental merit, a tribute to a hardier race of seafarers.

At one time no fisherman's back garden – a horticultural disaster area usually containing a rotting dinghy filled like some nightmare cornucopia with reeking fish-net, old tyres and a solitary gum-boot – was complete without an oily coat hung up to dry. Freshly coated with some disgusting tarry nostrum and with a broomstick through its outstretched arms, it swooped and banked in the wind, an eerie sight after dark. The lonely drunk tacking home up the street in the small hours was likely to have an occult experience that would leave him sober till his dying day. Putting in a tack from the bus shelter to the Wayside Pulpit he would be confronted by this great, black, headless goblin, its arms spread as it swooped and jigged in pursuit of its trembling prey.

'Back, back dangee!' the poor fellow would howl, clattering off in abject terror.

The sturdy traditional with neck-towel, body-and-soul lashings at ankle and cuff and the regulation two fingers lost off Cape Horn may have been replaced by the products of mad scientists chuckling over bubbling retorts but headgear remains a problem unsolved.

Your modern sou'wester is pathetic. It has a vestigial little scut of a tail designed for the sole purpose of funnelling water down your collar, unlike your old triple-stitched model, linseed oiled to the colour of game pie and drumming

in the wind like an Ulster marching band.

We are left with the *hood*. With your hood up its like trying to watch tennis from a sentry-box. You have to have the right complexion and profile to wear a hood. You may think that it lends you a pixie-like image but in fact you look like a ferret in a sack. So you leave it down and it fills with water and *then* you put it up. How about that for a spot of science?

t the tail-end of any Fastnet Race fleet there will be a round dozen clumbungay nohopers fighting their own little vendettas. The Admiral's Cuppers and other brand leaders have long since finished and are lying alongside while their crews are lying in the club bar. Meanwhile, back at Bishop's Rock deeds are being done.

We had been ding-donging with this other tortoise all the way from The Rock, we were past the Lizard and on the last leg – to put it ominously. At dusk the wind piped up from astern. We were both under spinnakers and steering like unicycles on ice. It piped up some more. Being unashamedly craven I suggested getting the kite down. The owner went all Empire on me. Eyeing our rival, still flying his, he said. 'Oh ho no. No. Ho ho no!' and went on in that vein.

We roared through the night and so did the other, half a cable to port. Being on the wheel was like having a sleeping polecat down your trousers – every move was made with exquisite caution. To have gybed would have gift-wrapped us in red and yellow nylon. We lost sight of our rival. I had my eyes closed. We blew out our spinnaker somewhere off Fowey.

We met up next day at Millbay Docks. 'You lot were bloody mad!' they told us, eyeing the scut of red and yellow at our masthead. We eyed the scut of blue and green at theirs. They followed our gaze.

'Our halyard was stuck', they said.

Flying a Kite

ather eyes a passing Admiral's Cupper with sour envy. To a man her crew wear sweatbands and their miniscule shorts bulge with muscle; they glare around through narrowed eyes. He steals an uncharitable glance at his own foredeck powerhouse.

There is brother-in-law Norman whose knobbly little knees give him the appearance of cane furniture – or, notes father, warming to his theme, in those bell-bottom shorts perhaps more like the bamboo and twin inverted flowerpot arrangement of an earwig trap. There is also Nance's boy with the jug ears and xylophone rib cage who is outgrowing his strength.

Setting a spinnaker with a crew of that calibre is not the sort of thing to be undertaken lightly. Yet some go for it in the same twice-a-summer spirit of devilry that prompts a garden barbecue. (It takes place the day after a three week heat-wave and it is enlivened by a thunderstorm, a dowsed grill and a power-cut.)

It would be better, muses father, if we had a twin-pole arrangement. They would be about as much use to him as a pair of stilts to a bandy-legged gardener. Father will hum-haw for an hour, staring up the mast as if in search of heavenly guidance. The burgee hangs limply, fishing smacks have bare steerage and ashore small leaves are stirring. By heaven he'll do it!

Mum, who doesn't give a tuppenny damn which sail is set is intent only upon tanning her spare tyre on the foredeck – it is an occupation which will stripe her horizontally in red and white, and which in (obsolete) buoyage terms will entitle mariners to pass her either to port or to starboard.

This privilege is roughly abused as the forehatch bursts open and father emerges, like some homely dung-beetle with its noisome prize, dragging the spinnaker bag.

'Oh you're not going to start fooling around with *that* thing!' she snarls. She reflects sourly that the cost of spinnaker, poles and snuffer is comparable to a holiday for two, somewhere hot.

There will follow half an hour of diligent activity with ropes and poles during which time the lee guy will be given a turn round the guardrail, ensuring a regular treat in store should anything as foolhardy as a gybe be attempted. Tension mounts as the time to *hoist and break out* approaches.

Like some failed conjuring trick a gaily coloured bundle jerks aloft. There are apolectic howls as it brushes the crosstrees. 'Sheet-sheet-sheet, guy-guy-guy!' screams father, leaping around. The bundle just *hangs* there in loops and swags like the lounge curtains. All it lacks is a pot-plant.

Setting a spinnaker is a defiance of fate. Aladdin, having blown down the spout of his Wonderful Lamp teapot fashion, need hardly be surprised at the emergence of the genie mopping its eyes and vowing vengance.

After much jerking around at pole and sheet the sail fills, staggering up as though it had just fallen off its bike. All stand back in admiration. Photos are taken. Lunch is dismissed with a scornful wave of the hand. Half an hour later and with upraised moistened forefinger to assess wind strength, father decides that it must be handed. Smacks may not as yet be making for harbour and whole trees are not yet in motion but one cannot be too careful. 'Let's show 'em how to do it,' he declares unwisely.

'A nice quick drop then!' he encourages – a condemned man instructing his executioner. To ensure a total disaster he puts Norman on the halyard and nominates Graham to the crucial task of letting fly and gathering in. With these two flop-heads involved it is tantamount to leaving a brimming bucket of whitewash in a day nursery. Graham furrows a neanderthal brow. He dimly remembers that the last time he went sailing it was the *red* corner that had to be unclipped . . . .

The advent of the Spi-squeezer or spinnaker sock should have robbed the sail of all threat, but this piece of hosiery has all the potential for surprise of a king cobra in a Christmas stocking. A thunderhead is building up but father is of the opinion that it will mean a short shower at worst. The yacht is suddenly over on her ear. A half-snuffed spinnaker is galloping around aloft like some gigantic bumblebee when the downhaul snaps ..... the yacht roars downwind and upriver. 'It says here that the swingbridge only opens on Wednesdays!' notes mum with the pilotbook triumphantly.

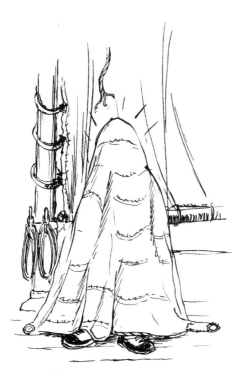

If the setting and lowering of spinnakers is vulnerable to the ham-fisted then the *bagging* of one down below while leaping to windward in the unrated, unbelievable and unthinkable cruiser race is rich ground for ten-thumbed ineptitude. The saloon is swathed in a colourful ballooning mass like some vast meringue in which two wan-faced workers swim desperately. They are stuffing it back in its bag along with a washing up towel, a wet sock, two pairs of knickers and a cheese and tomato sandwich. Later, as the windward mark is rounded, the sail will soar aloft in a symbolic wineglass shape, distributing largesse like a Maundy ceremonial. Muriel, who won't-be-spoken-to-like-that quits the tiller and flounces below tight of lip and that's all she's taking.

For that doyen of gaff rig, Old Harry, and despite the fact

that his topsail sets like a rag rug over a clothes line, the carrying of what he terms 'fancy stuff' becomes an art form. Onlookers shade their eyes as first one and then another dun-coloured, wrinkled and shapeless bundle of canvas inches aloft.

These moorakers, bonnets and Jimmy Greens (to use the proper nomenclature) have all seen service in other roles. British Road Services, proclaims the topsail, Haywards Calf Meal announces the flying staysail perplexingly. This sail, set in stops, bursts into shape at the tug of a sheet, showering those on deck with a bonanza of spiders and pipe dottle.

Old Harry's converted eel-wrangler, when laid alongside, becomes a place of pilgrimage for students of traditional sail. Antiquarians cluster on the quayside. They note with approval that the owner still has his little iron bumkin and that his dandywink is in working order. Two maiden ladies from Crewe, down for the ozone and potted shrimps, listen in mounting alarm.

'I'd love to watch him tripping his fid!' notes an onlooker, disturbingly. He gazes aloft in contemplation of this rich spectacle.

For the owners of gaffers the setting of topsails is *de rigueur*, like the wearing of grey spats at a posh wedding. Novice owners, new to gaff, adopt this responsibility with dry mouth and pounding heart. Topsails go shimmying up and down masts inverted and sideways like targets at a fun-fair. An orgy of photography accompanies success. Prints will show an acreage of mainsail topped by a brown smear in similar fashion to family snaps of auntie in her deckchair with gargantuan kneecaps and a miniature head.

An increase of wind strength from Force 1–3 (whole twigs in motion) gingers father into action.

'All hands to take in topsail!' he howls pointblank at Nance, coincidental with the appearance on deck of tea and biscuits. He then makes the gross error of appointing Graham as helmsman. Mother Theresa might have been a safer bet had that good woman been available. Graham

whose grasp of practical seamanship is limited to the
bunny-hole-and-tree method of tying a bowline, is ready for
his finest hour. Reliable hands have been stationed at halyard, sheet and downhaul ready for a quick drop.

'When I nod my head give me a quick shake,' instructs
father revealing a sorry trust in human nature and
Graham's in particular.

'Like this uncle?' says that cretin, wagging his great daft
poll.

'NO BOY,' thunders Father, Like *this*...nodding with
vigour.

A barbed wire fence could be fed into a combine harvester
with less dire effect than what follows. Graham bangs the
helm hard over. Jib and staysail go hard a'back and three
reliable hands release their grips. Like some monster skylark

the topsail, tethered only by its sheet which has taken a turn around the end of the gaff, wings aloft into that great azure bowl on beating pinions. The flogging mainsheet snares and triggers off the liferaft just as the coil slides overboard. With masterly ill-timing Graham hits the engine starter button. GLUMP says the engine, stopping dead.

Father is on his hands and knees thumping his head on the deck. 'I''m going to kill him!' he chuckles eerily, 'I'm going to kill him!'

suppose the sheer naked animal power of the modern auxilliary engine has exacerbated things. I grew up with the view that an engine was a sort of bonus, like a Maundy purse for which one should drop a curtsy. You mumbled along in a flat calm thankfully enough but you never expected your engine to get you out of trouble. You didn't know it was running unless you clapped an ear to the deck and signalled for silence.

'Looking to see if the water was coming out' was the prime responsibility of sailing wives. Imagine driving a car and having to urge your wife out in the rain to look at the exhaust! 'There's smoke coming out dear.' Oh good.

Going astern was something else. We used to tow dinghies in those days. The quay wall begins to loom up beyond the bowsprit. The skippers's eyes begin to pop. Bang goes the lever full astern. Nothing happens. Then, like some lost lambkin seeking its dam, the dinghy nods and hurries alongside. Silence except for stertorous breathing.

I had a boat with a converted Austin Seven engine. The gear lever worked back to front. The man who bought her from me came back from his first cruise with his bowsprit end red with brick dust. 'How far did you get?' I asked. 'Across the jetty and into the pub privvy,' he snarled.

A Little Touch Astern

he prospect of manoeuvring under engine within the narrow confines of harbour or marina is one which keeps many a novice owner uneasy in his bed. 'You should never have had the rissoles', his wife accuses, bouncing steadily on her side of the mattress as he revolves unendingly on his. Should I put the helm hard over and open the throttle wide or should I go ahead-and-astern? he agonises. Either option promises to be richly rewarding for onlookers.

Of course, yachting writers write copiously on the subject. 'Do you know your turning circle?' they sneer, drawing one in dotted lines in case somebody doesn't know what a circle looks like. 'Once you know your turning circle you can proceed with confidence. Having started your turn *do not waver*,' they encourage. In other words if you are going to hit the refuelling barge, hit it head on and hit it *hard*.

The fact that turning circles are usually banana-shaped and alter in size according to wind, current and the apoplectic screams of the Harbour Master tends to escape the notice of the writer at the helm of a word processor. They have not as yet even considered the effects of the dreaded astern gear.

Father commences his turn relaxed and smiling. He has visited this marina before and his manoeuvre on that occasion was a little gem and subject for admiring congratulations from all sides. His hand rests lightly upon the helm. Then at some point while approaching the apogee of his (eliptical) circle his knuckles whiten, his eyeballs begin to protrude like church mission coatpegs and his smile becomes the mirthless rictus of a rocking horse. His pipestem snaps like a dry twig. He chickens out and bangs the gear lever from full ahead to hard astern. 'Wheee!' howls the gearbox. 'Ooooo!' exclaim the onlookers in excited anticipation.

Father's modest intention had been to berth his boat smoothly and efficiently with minimum fuss, quiet and unhurried, *professionally*. Had he entered harbour dressed as a hobby-horse and blowing a cardboard trumpet he could hardly have attracted more unwanted attention. From the Harbour Office a loudhailer crackles into life. 'Harrump, gag, dronkit gondrome!' it roars commandingly. Our mariner at this point has his vessel wind-up-tail and in the narrow bit. She is revolving prior to going into the dreaded zig-zags. Mother, knowing the signs, has gone below to put the brussels sprouts on.

It is always unnerving, while carrying out a manoeuvre, to note what people ashore are doing. If it is going well then very likely nobody will notice the fact. When pedestrians suddenly stop and shade their eyes, when shopkeepers come to stand in their doorways, and when the cockpits of moored yachts suddenly fill with spectators it is high time to do something drastic like clutching the throat and falling to the deck with rolling eyeballs or handing over the con to Percy. 'I mustn't hog the helm. Here lad, try your hand at a simple manoeuvre.

Engine manufacturers seem to be bent upon unsettling the mariner's already shaky confidence. 'When did you last dip your sump...? renew your impeller...? replace your filters eh, EH? Tell me that! And *how about your alternator belt?*' they sneer with mirthless laughter.

The owner is hell-bent for the open lock gate with a following wind – the lockmaster waving two-handed from his window. The owner's hand hovers above the gear lever as if about to detonate a factory chimney – a spectacle which the ensuing fracas will resemble closely.

Perhaps the keenest test of equanimity is the auxilliary engine which has to be stopped and then started again to achieve reverse gear. It is like asking a tightrope walker to produce his bus pass when halfway across Niagara Falls. He stops, lays down his balancing pole, begins patting pockets. 'I have it here . . . somewheeeeeeeahhh . . !'

Undeniably efficient though these small motors may be, the brief interval of silence between off and on again is no time for social intercourse. There is an intake of breath. It fires! Breath whistles out again like a punctured air-bed.

Over-confidence wreaks its own dire punishment and the gear lever imposes it. A stately procession of Cardinals, under full sail and approaching a rag rug on a polished parquet floor promises a spectacle of equal interest to father *who likes to brief his crew in advance* of a manoeuvre.

'I shall circle once to assess the situation and then lay my port side to,' he explains, implying that he will do so person-ally and alone, levitating perhaps or maybe skimming round in a yogic flight with knees akimbo. He then proceeds to do something entirely different. It is a situation akin to an ant's nest disturbed by the gardener's fork. Tiny creatures clutch-ing eggs hurry hither and yon in fear and panic. Crew, clutching fenders, scuttle to and fro across the coachroof with comparable urgency.

The ultimate test of nerve and skill is to lay alongside the fuelling berth just after the lock gates have opened. For the tyro it is a folly as rich in potential disaster as attempting an after diner speech, owlish on club claret, and containing the words 'auspicious occasion'.

The aim is to hover ready to make a dive for the berth as soon as the present incumbent quits it. Half a dozen yachts circle very slowly while half a dozen wives hiss instructions from as many companionways. 'NOW Gerald!' rasps a voice. Then the boatowner in the berth decides to take on water as well and too late, too late Gerald (who has gunned his engine) hits the astern gear. Saint Peter, patron saint of boatmen, places hand over eyes and shudders.

Dead astern a vast powerboat bubbles and burbles like simmering porridge. High on her flying bridge stands her owner wearing a paisley cravat of pneumatic perfection. Father, looking up his nostrils with distaste, also wears a cravat. His looks like a surgical dressing.

The tremendous thirst of twin what-ever-they-areas will mean a top of commensurate size for the fuel attendant. Father will want a five-gallon top-up dribbled in as though administering ear-drops. He gets the blind eye treatment. He won't be treated like that! By God no! He'll go somewhere else won't he! Like rowing ashore with a jerrycan when the tank ran dry. Two miles through drizzle then bleeding the engine when he got back. THAT showed 'em.

A series of shattering bangs and barking mechanical eructations heralds the arrival under power of Old Harry in his converted whelk pilliker. Lacking the refinement of a gearbox Old Harry relies upon his own unique sense of judgement when approaching a berth, stopping his thumping monolith with a screwdriver across plug and block and carrying his considerable way thereafter in total silence.

In World War 2 the arrival of the dreaded 'buzz-bomb' was typified by the cut-out of its throaty growl – silence – and then a mighty explosion. This eerie silence followed by detonation also typifies Old Harry's arrival in the berth of his choice.

Like rabbits mesmerised by a stoat, yacht crews destined to receive this horrific visitor watch saucer-eyed. A pitchpine bowsprit like some witch doctor's accusing finger points unerringly. 'It could be YOU!' it seems to proclaim. Then comes frantic activity as a wealth of fenders are produced. Old Harry's rope-clad motor tyres promise little comfort. Chins are squared. Men stand ready with little tubular boathooks and one crew jumps ship *en bloc* lead by a junoesque lady who looks like a Samurai warrior in her foundation garments.

The Harbour Master, who had rashly declared that Old Harry would enter the marina under sail 'Over my dead body' was later coaxed out from under his desk with a chocolate bourbon. He was sparing in his comments. 'Mummy, mummy!' he lisped crawling back again.

Let yachting writers have the last word (they will anyway). The effects of a contra-turning propeller are lucidly explained with diagram, song and dance. 'Know your propeller torque,' they rattle. 'Will she throw her stern to port when going astern?' It is a rhetorical question akin to criticising a woman's pastry. What they *don't* explain is how to get out of the dreaded zig-zags.

Attempting to turn 180 degrees in a narrow waterway by alternately going ahead and astern leads, inevitably, to an agonising sideways progress down wind. Owners of other boats watch triumphantly. 'Poor devil . . . !' they gloat, wincing as a bow pulpit suddenly rears up like a praying mantis. Apart from fasting, abstinence and the taking of Holy Orders there is no cure. Remote monastic retreats are full of ex-owners clutching gear levers.